D1479438

FLYING LEGENDS

Color Photography John M. Dibbs

Written by Tony Holmes

MBI Publishing Company

For the quiet genius of my Father, the love that is my Mother and for Pam who is my reason to be. Always.

This edition published in 1998 by MBI Publishing Company, 729 Prospect Avenue, PO Box 1, Osceola, WI 54020-0001 USA

Previously published by The Plane Picture Company, 35-37, The High Street, Wheathampstead, Hertfordshire, AL4 8BB, England
Schück Verlag, CH-8134, Adliswil, Switzerland

Originally published in English and German by The Plane Picture Company and Schück Publishing

Flying Legends
© John Dibbs

All rights reserved. With the exception of quoting brief passages for the purposes of review no part of this publication may be reproduced without prior written permission from the Publisher.

The information in this book is true and complete to the best of our knowledge. All recommendations are made without any guarantee on the part of the author or Publisher, who also disclaim any liability incurred in connection with the use of this data or specific details.

We recognize that some words, model names and designations, for example, mentioned herein are the property of the trademark holder. We use them for identification purposes only. This is not an official publication.

MBI Publishing Company books are also available at discounts in bulk quantity for industrial or sales-promotional use. For details write to Special Sales Manager at Motorbooks International Wholesalers & Distributors, 729 Prospect Avenue, PO Box 1, Osceola, WI 54020-0001 USA.
John Dibbs shot all the color images in this book on Fuji transparency stock rated at 50 and 100ASA.
Camera equipment: Canon E0S1 and F-1, using Canon and Sigma lenses. Camera holdalls supplied by Camera Care Systems. Film Processing: PDQ Laboratories. Authentic WW2 Flying Jackets - Real McCoys (New Zealand)

ACKNOWLEDGEMENTS
The color photographs that comprise this book are the result of many peoples' hard work, dedication, good will (and good faith), and not least generosity. Special thanks go to:
The Fighter Collection, The Old Flying Machine Company, The Aircraft Restoration Company, Planes of Fame Air Museum, The British Aerial Museum, The Alpine Fighter Collection, The Shuttleworth Collection, The Imperial War Museum, 'Black Six' Restoration Team, B-17 Preservation Ltd, The Battle of Britain Memorial Flight, Frasca International, The Duke of Brabant Air Force, The Intrepid Aviation Company, The Squadron, Santa Monica Museum of Flying, The Scandinavian Historic Flight, Polar Air Museum, 'Weary Warriors' B-25, Personal Plane Services, Dick Hansen, Vlado Lenoch Dave King - Canon (UK), Graham Armitage - Sigma (UK), Peter Bowerman - CCS

Thanks also to **Aeroplane Monthly, Jeff Ethell, Bruce Robertson** and **Jerry Scutts** for furnishing the archive black and white photographs included in this volume. Introduction photography: **Terry Galvin, Lane End Studios**
Thanks to AVM Cliff Spink & staff at RAF Bentley Priory, HQ No. 11 Group

Library of Congress Cataloging-in-Publication Data Available
ISBN 0-7603-0563-3

Concept and color photography by **John M. Dibbs**
Written by **Tony Holmes**
Page design by **Karen Baker**
Reproduction by **Graphic Techniques, Eastcote, England**
Printed in China through **World Print Ltd.**

The Plane Picture Company

CONTENTS

FOREWORD

The question of selecting my favourite wartime fighter aircraft is not easy. Aircraft in my opinion are like the opposite sex. Machine or human being, none has it all!

Having been trained before the war in the University of London Air Squadron by RAF flying instructors, I was seventy five per-cent ready for combat flying, and was sent to the Royal Air Force at Cranwell to complete my flying education.

Leaving Cranwell, I was ordered to proceed to Duxford to join 66 Fighter Squadron, equipped with Spitfires. Here I learned the hard way the merits of this lovely little fighter. Up to this point I had only flown slow biplane machines with a top speed of about 130mph. Nor had I ever flown an aircraft with flaps or retractable undercarriage. My new commanding officer was angry that he had been sent a pilot with experience only on antiquated aircraft. His other problem was that he had no such aeroplane as an AT-6 Harvard to convert me over to the Spitfire Mark I. Eventually he made me sit in the cockpit of a Spitfire to memorise all the various controls and instruments, and then I was off into the blue.

The sensitivity of this viceless little fighter helped me through an hour's enchanting flying, then I was back on the ground in one piece.

Alas, my happiness was short lived. After about a month the C.O. sent for me to say that some stupid secretary at the Air Ministry had mistyped my orders and that I should have gone to 56 Squadron, and not 66 Squadron. 56 Squadron was equipped with Hawker Hurricanes. Despite leaving my beloved Spitfires, I was pleased to be going to an airfield which would undoubtedly be in the heavy aerial fighting when it came.

My arrival at '56' was uneventful. The Squadron had flown away North for a week's gunnery practice. The Engineering Officer who had remained at base approached me. "There's a new replacement Hurricane that needs flight testing. Could you do that please?" So off I went to fly another type of aircraft.

An hour or so later I landed, having fallen in love with this beauty as well. Although slower in the climb, she had a tighter turning circle and better aileron response. I was not unhappy.

Shot down in flames in the Battle of Britain, I retired to hospital for two years of painful plastic surgery. This was compensated for the fact that I had performed reasonably in the defence of my country. Returning to flying in 1943 on a Spitfire squadron, I was impressed by the increased performance of the Spitfire V over the earlier Mark I's, which I had originally flown.

I then volunteered to join the North African campaign. The heat of the North African sun soon proved too much for my newly acquired skin grafts, and I returned to England.

On arrival in Britain I was sent to the Air Fighting Development Unit. This organisation was equipped with at least one of each of the fighter aircraft being flown by the Allies:- Spitfires, Hurricanes, P-47 Thunderbolt, P-51, Mosquito, etc. We had three P-51's, two powered with Allison engines and the third with the Rolls Royce Merlin engine. The 'Allison' Mustang was a good aeroplane, but when powered with the R.R. Merlin, it became a delight.

Looking back over the years, I recall these three aeroplanes, which I flew in combat, and they above all fill my mind with warm happy memories. To have been a fighter pilot in the Royal Air Force during World War II left one with no further ambitions. I suppose in a small way one was conscious of fighting for King and Country, personally I flew and fought to keep the adrenaline pumping hard.

Geoffrey Page

Wg Cdr Geoffrey Page DSO OBE DFC*

INTRODUCTION

As one currently privileged to demonstrate many of the famous World War II combat aircraft, I remain in awe of the design genius, the skill of those who built and maintained them and amazed at the ability and courage of the young men and women who tested, flew and fought with these legendary 'planes.

In the heat of that worldwide conflict, enormous advances were made in aerodynamics, armament and production-engineering. The piston engine was pushed to the outer-edge of materials and combustion-engineering sciences. The boundaries of compressibility and the sub-stratosphere were probed. The capacity of man was taken to its limits.

These aircraft are of great historical importance. They were the last of the 'chivalric', man-to-man, 'engines of war'. After these phenomenal propeller-driven aeroplanes came the jet and guided-missile age. Mass-produced in tens of thousands to defend, and end, the world's last global conflict, these great propeller combat types represent the zenith and the end of a technology.

The remaining flying tributes to that incredible period are few and cherished. History is kept alive, in the restoration, maintenance and flight of these now rare and eminent aircraft. More than half-a-century after conception, their sight, emotional sounds and terrible beauty are preserved for the education and appreciation of later generations. Modern care, capital and dedication will take them forward to posterity.

The splendid images we enjoy in this fine book, captured by the lens of John Dibbs, demonstrate not only his application and abundant talent, but also give you a glimpse of the power, the glory and the soaring majesty of these Flying Legends.

Stephen Grey

The Fighter Collection, Duxford

November 1996

Imagine my surprise to be invited to England to participate in the world famous 'Flying Legends' airshow at Duxford.

Imagine my astonishment and pride to discover the care and outstanding workmanship lavished on the very Hellcat in which I had scored seven of my first nine victories over 50 years ago, when I was a young man flying off an aircraft carrier in the Pacific.

To see history preserved with such dedication within one's lifetime is to renew one's faith in mankind and to revive the hope that the world will never again fall into international conflict.

The photographs in this book, not to speak of those of my 'old bird', are magnificent. I commend you to pass a copy to a friend. It is as close as one can get to the emotion of these wonderful aircraft, without touching, hearing and seeing them fly during 'Legends' at Duxford.

Treasure this one of a kind book. Good Luck to you all.

Alex Vraciu

Alex Vraciu

Cdr Alex Vraciu USN

onflict, and the threat of it, has acted as the catalyst in the never-ending search for the perfect weapons of war. Military aggression spurs on technological progress, and that fact has never been better illustrated than in the 21 years of uneasy peace enjoyed globally between 1918 and 1939. At the end of the Great War the most effective tool in the Allied arsenal was the aircraft. It had been developed in four short, but bloody, years from the role of 'bit part player', acting as a spotting aid for the artillery, into a strategic bomber that could cause more damage in a single raid than the largest field piece.

Just as the multi-engined types had been developed into the 'dreadnoughts' of the skies, so fighters too had evolved from being the converted liaison types of 1914, whose offensive weaponry comprised a revolver or rifle wielded by the pilot, into highly manoeuvrable, fast and well-armed pursuit machines, capable of achieving a modicum of air superiority over the frontline.

With the cessation of hostilities on 11 November 1918, and the signing of the Treaty of Versailles the following year, the requirement for more advanced fighters and bombers evaporated almost overnight, and the major air arms of the world were forced to 'make do' through the employment of war-surplus types whose designs dated back to the mid-war period. Tired of conflict and bankrupt from funding vast armies, the governments of the key European powers in Britain and France enforced draconian cuts in the size of their armed forces. For example, the RAF was pruned from a strength of 188 squadrons and 291,000 men in November 1918, to just 25 squadrons and 28,300 men by March 1920.

In this environment of negative growth within the air forces of the major powers, many aircraft manufacturers focused on the fledgling air transport market in order to remain

afloat. In an effort to bestow upon their machines a useful range when carrying a payload of people and mail, rather than bombs, manufacturers turned to companies like Bristol, Napier, Rolls-Royce and Curtiss to furnish them with more powerful, and reliable, engines. Although the rotary had reigned supreme during much of World War 1, it had reached the limits of its development by 1918. Far greater bhp figures were now being achieved with water-cooled inline and air-cooled radial engines.

Whilst the transportation of people provided the impetus – and cash – for companies to continue to produce more advanced bombers for military service throughout the austere 1920s, no such carrot was dangled in the face of prospective fighter manufacturers. Therefore, no new designs entered service until 1922-24, and even these machines relied strongly on wartime design traits. Small numbers of biplane fighters were periodically ordered by the major powers throughout the remaining years of the 1920s and

into the 1930s, thus ensuring a steady rise in the performance of these types.

With the world gripped by an economic depression, Europe enjoyed an uneasy peace and the USA pursued a policy of isolationism. There was little impetus to improve weapons of war, and aircraft in particular, but this did not deter a handful of pioneering individuals who looked for more peaceful applications for their engineering brilliance. Air racing became a popular

Air Chief Marshal Sir Hugh Dowding

▲ *Battle of Britain Memorial Window, Bentley Priory*

▶ *ACM Dowding's Desk No.11 Group HQ, Bentley Priory*

SLDR DOUGLAS BADER. D.S.O.&D.F.C. 242. (CANADIAN) SQUADRON

outlet for performance aeronautics, with the famed series of Schneider Trophy events for floatplanes up to 1931 providing a crucial testing ground for new monoplane designs incorporating high-revving liquid-cooled inline engines and stressed-skin airframes.

Rolls-Royce had learned much through air racing, and it was one of their products which powered arguably the first really advanced all-British design to enter RAF service since the end of the Great War. Hawker's Hart bomber of 1928 combined revolutionary streamlining and a V12 inline Kestrel engine that cranked out nearly 500 hp. The overall shape of the powerplant allowed company aerodynamicists to produce an aircraft that could achieve speeds 10 mph faster than the RAF's fighter of the day, the Bristol Bulldog.

It was only a matter of time before the Hart sired a single-seat fighter derivative, and in 1931 the Fury was ordered into series production. Powered by the uprated Kestrel II.S engine, the aircraft was the first production fighter in the world to be able to achieve 200 mph in level flight.

The advent of the Hart had sounded alarm bells within the RAF's high command, who realised that the fighter of the late 1930s would have to be able to attain speeds in excess of 250 mph, and be armed with four machine-guns. No designs were even on the drawing board that could fulfil these criteria at the time of the Hawker bomber's service debut. Nevertheless, in 1930 the Air Ministry issued Specification F.7/30 which covered the acquisition of just such a machine, and offered manufacturers the reward of substantial production orders for the winning design.

The relaxed pace that had been adopted by the Air Ministry in re-equipping the RAF in the interwar period dramatically quickened as a result of events unfolding in Germany in 1933. The National Socialist (Nazi) Party had seized power legitimately through the general election of July 1932, and once their leader, Adolf Hitler succeeded the ageing Hindenburg as Chancellor the following year, he rapidly set about re-arming the crestfallen nation. From an aeronautical point of view, German manufacturers had remained active in the 1920s building transport aircraft, and this experience with multi-engined, all-metal types was put to effective use once the country freed itself from the shackles of the Treaty of Versailles in 1934.

Other key nations in Europe commenced drastic re-equipment programmes in light of Germany's sudden militaristic turn, pouring money and manpower into the production of better fighters and bombers. Across the globe, Japan now also started to flex its muscles in defiance of the League of Nations over land it had seized in Manchuria. Although still espousing neutrality, and not immediately threatened by Europe due to its geographical positioning, the USA was nevertheless concerned by Japan's rumblings in light of their interests in the Philippines and Hawaii. The USAAC and the US Navy therefore issued a whole host of new requirements in the mid-1930s for designs that would take advantage of the most up-to-date technologies then available.

Hawker Hind

Back in Britain the advent of Bristol's privately funded Type 142 in 1934 had further inspired the nation's fighter manufacturers into feverish action in search of the 250 mph+ interceptor. With bombers now cruising at speeds nearing 280 mph, the RAF realised that its F.7/30 specification would leave them with a fighter ill-equipped to deal with marauding monoplane bombers sent across the waves to strike at Britain from the continent.

The Air Ministry therefore tailored its requirements to suit two promising prototype fighters then emerging, one from Hawkers – F.36/34 covering their design – and Supermarine, which adopted the spec F.37/34. Both aircraft were of monoplane configuration, which was a radical departure for the RAF, who had mistrusted the single wing layout since the highly advanced Bristol M.1C had suffered numerous structural failures whilst in service during the Great War. With the advent of new manufacturing techniques, aeronautical engineers at last proved to the air force that single-wing aircraft were as strong, if not stronger, than biplane designs.

The RAF also stipulated that the armament of the new fighters had to be doubled from four to eight machine-guns, and that they had to have a top speed in excess of 300 mph. Fortunately for Hawkers and Supermarine, Rolls-Royce had been keeping abreast of developments and had further improved, and enlarged, their Kestrel engine into what would eventually become the Merlin. With a power output of 1000 hp, the engine gave the new prototypes an unmatched power-to-weight ratio that allowed them to accommodate the increased armament without detrimentally affecting the types' performance.

The first RAF squadrons to receive the new monoplane fighters began re-equipping in 1937-38. During the last four years of peace the air force had literally trebled in size, with new monoplane aircraft replacing the old biplane types. Aircrew training also increased its output to satisfy demand, new bases were opened all across the country and advanced technology in the form of radar was incorporated into tracking sites constructed along the vulnerable south-east coastline.

Although the British programme of rearmament was implemented swiftly, German re-equipment easily outstripped all efforts by the RAF. A new crop of aircraft were being issued at breakneck speed to the Luftwaffe from manufacturers like Junkers, Heinkel, Dornier and, most importantly, Messerschmitt. Like other prominent weapons utilised by the Germans in the first year of war, the latter company's Bf 109 got the chance to prove itself in combat in Spain from late 1936. New types and new tactics were tested in this bitter two-year war, and the overwhelming superiority of German combat aircraft played a

Bristol Blenheim Mk I directly developed from the privately funded Bristol type 142

significant part in securing victory for General Franco. Likewise, Japanese forces also got to experience the crucible of war following their invasion of China in 1937, although the opposition initially encountered by the Army Air Force and Imperial Navy was negligible.

By the summer of 1939 all the key types that would fight for supremacy of the skies over Europe were in frontline service with the Allied and Axis air arms. Across the Atlantic, the USAAC and US Navy were also on the cusp of receiving monoplane fighters and bombers that would be in the thick of the action following the raid on Pearl Harbor in December 1941.

As the most advanced instruments of conflict yet seen over the battlefield, these aircraft ranged against each other by the Allied and Axis alliances helped revolutionise warfare in the first two years of World War 2. Combat evolved from the static trench slog in the fields of mud that so symbolised the Great War two decades earlier, into a lightning invasion (*Blitzkrieg*) across enemy territory, although dominance in the air was necessary to facilitate any such advance. The role of the aircraft would continue to grow in importance as the war ground on, and the evolution of monoplane combat types, principally through the advent of more powerful engines, is graphically shown in the pages of this volume, which serves as a tribute to the Flying Legends of World War 2.

Hawker
HURRICANE

'The Hawker fighter had already earned a formidable reputation from the summer of 1940, and as a young man, with the government providing me with a high-performance aircraft in which to hone my skills, it was a privilege to fly the Hurricane. Its Battle of Britain top scoring achievement inspired us all.' **Plt Off Bill Bedford, No 9 SFTS, Hullavington, 1941**

Long remembered as the 'other fighter' of the Battle of Britain, the Hurricane was a benchmark design not only for its manufacturer, but more importantly for its principal employer, the Royal Air Force. With the arrival of the first Mk Is at Northolt for No 111 Sqn in December 1937, the RAF had finally made the jump from biplane to monoplane fighter – and as world events less than two years later would graphically show, not a moment too soon.

Between the wars, fighter design had progressed steadily, if rather slowly, in Britain as the biplane concept was refined into its purest form. Gloster and Hawker were the principal manufacturers of single-seat fighters for the air force, with designs like the Woodcock, Gamecock, Gauntlet and Gladiator featuring heavily in the frontline ranks. Painted silver, and decorated with heraldic squadron colours, these biplane fighters could trace their lineage directly back to the Camels and SE5As of the Great War. One type, however, embodied a more forward looking approach to its construction, and thanks to its use of an inline engine, was capable of previously unheard of speeds for a biplane. That aircraft was the Hawker Fury I, which boasted a top speed of over 200 mph. Designed by Sir Sydney Camm, the fighter's internal construction of light alloy and steel tube comprised four longerons, internally wire-braced. This structure was renowned for both its simplicity of construction and rugged durability.

The Hurricane owes much to the Fury (and the Hind family of bombers which essentially spawned the biplane fighter) in respect to its internal layout and powerplant. Camm had realised that the natural progression of fighter technology would see the monoplane design in service before the end of the 1930s, and therefore set out to steal a march on his competitors. Using the Fury/Rolls-Royce Goshawk (later replaced by the all-

new Merlin) combination as a basis, the Hawker prototype was viewed with such hope by the Air Ministry that Specification F.36/34 was drawn up around it. On 6 November 1935 the prototype completed its first flight, and from that point on rapid progress was made.

The fighter soon exceeded even the most optimistic high-speed performance predictions, and on the strength of this, the Air Ministry placed an initial order for 600 aircraft on 3 June 1936. Toting eight .303 in machine guns, and powered by a state of the art Merlin II engine that propelled it along at speeds well in excess of 300 mph, the Hurricane I was the most advanced design of its type in the world when issued to Fighter Command in late 1937.

By the time Europe erupted into war in September 1939, 19 frontline units were equipped with the Hawker fighter, and it wasn't long before the type was thrust into combat. During the Battle of France the Hurricane acquitted itself well in the face of overwhelming odds, and although British pilots admitted that the Bf 109E was superior to their mount in terms of speed in the dive, they were happy to engage in a turning fight with the Luftwaffe's premier fighter. The Battle of Britain saw no less than 32 squadrons of Hurricanes (compared with 19 of Spitfires) committed to the last-ditch defence of the 'Sceptred Isle', and the type soon gained an enviable reputation as a steady gun platform – it could also absorb an astounding amount of damage.

In late 1940 production switched to the re-engined Mark II, fitted with the uprated Merlin XX powerplant and improved armament. Declared obsolescent in the fighter role by mid-1941, Hurricane IIs continued to see much service across the globe in the ground attack and close support roles, with the venerable Hawker fighter still gainfully employed performing this vital task in the Far East up to VJ-Day.

▲ Armourers bomb up a Hurricane Mk II of No 402 Sqn at RAF Warmwell in late 1941

▶ Hurricane Mk Is of No 111 Sqn at RAF Northolt in early 1939

'On 11 September 1940 I flew up to Martlesham Heath from Biggin Hill to take over command on No 257 Sqn, which was flying Hurricanes, and was greeted on the tarmac by my old friend Flt Lt Pete Brothers, who was one of the flight commanders. I bade farewell to my lovely Spitfires, which I had flown for some 1000 hours, and walked over to my new Hurricane with Pete, who was going to fill me in on the cockpit drill and flying characteristics. I had never been very close to a Hurricane before, let alone sat in the cockpit. Hurricane P4190 sat there on its wide, sturdy, undercarriage, with its slightly hunched, crouching appearance. I was not very impressed, as it looked like a great sturdy carthorse compared with my Spit, which was like a racing thoroughbred.'

Sqn Ldr Bob Stanford Tuck, OC No 257 Sqn, Martlesham Heath, 1940

Hurricane Mk IIC ▲

Hurricane Mk XII ▶

▲ Hurricane Mk I L1547 in February 1938

▶ Hurricane Mk XII

'I had just lined up on a Junkers Ju 88 in the middle of the rear formation, but was still out of range, when a Bf 109 above and behind me opened up and tracer stabbed past my aircraft. There was a bang in the cockpit – a bullet had shattered the side panel of the windscreen. There was nothing to do but slam the stick hard over and turn in towards him in a steep turn, as he flashed past going very fast. My number two, Carl Capon, weaved behind me and kept station perfectly. With Carl weaving furiously behind me, I saw below me and to my left the great phalanx of German bombers ploughing ahead. Fortunately, the rest of the formation of my Hurricanes was now joining battle, together with the Spitfires, slicing in like a school of sharks.'

Sqn Leader Bob Stanford Tuck, OC No 257 Sqn, Martlesham Heath, 1940

▲ Hurricane Mk IIC has its cannon reloaded

◀ Hurricane Mk IIC

▶ Hurricane Mk IIC

'In the Hurricane we knew that the Me 109 could out-dive us, but not out-turn us. With that knowledge, one obviously used the turn manoeuvre rather than trying to beat the man at the game in which he was clearly superior. With a '109 sitting behind you, you'd stay in a really tight turn, and after a few turns the position would be reversed and you'd be on his tail. In short, I'd say that the Hurricane was a magnificent aeroplane to go to war in.'
Plt Off Geoffrey Page, No 56 Sqn, North Weald, 1940

'After the first day's combat with my new squadron in the Hurricane, my first impressions of this magnificent aircraft were completely wiped out, as I realised the sterling qualities of its handling. It had not a vice in its whole make-up. Its wonderful visibilty forward over the nose, considering the great Rolls-Royce Merlin engine in front, and its remarkable steadiness and solidness when the eight guns crashed into life made it an absolute delight to fly, but I would have liked more speed. I felt sure that if under heavy attack, it was capable of taking tremendous punishment, and this later proved to be the case.'

Sqn Ldr Bob Stanford Tuck, OC No 257 Sqn, Martlesham Heath, 1940

'I write about the Hurricane with admiration and affection, tinged with a little sorrow. In a way it was sad that this great old war-horse was put in the shade by its successor. The beautiful Spitfire immediately took the limelight and even took the credit for winning the Battle of Britain, in which there were far more Hurricanes involved than Spitfires. Of course the Spitfire was a lovely plane, combining speed, manoeuvrability and beauty. But let's not forget the old Hurricane, as those of us who flew it never will. She forgave many mistakes that the Spitfire wouldn't, both in the air and on the ground, and in the early days, when we took to the air with so little experience, we needed a lot of forgiveness.'
Flg Off Jim Goodson, No 71 'Eagle' Sqn, Martlesham Heath, 1941

▲ Hurricane Mk IIC

▶ Sea Hurricane Mk I

Vickers-Supermarine
SPITFIRE

'Lovely to look at, delightful to fly, the Spitfire became the pride and joy of thousands of young men from practically every country in what, then, constituted the free world.' **Grp Capt Hugh 'Cocky' Dundas**

The only British fighter to remain in production throughout World War 2, the exploits of the Vickers-Supermarine Spitfire are legendary. Over 22,500 were produced in mark numbers ranging from I through to 24, this total also including over 1000 built as dedicated Seafire fleet fighters for the Royal Navy. Following on from his successes with the Schneider Trophy racing seaplanes of the 1920s and 30s, Reginald J. Mitchell designed the Spitfire in response to ever more challenging Air Ministry requirements. The prototype, K5054 first took to the skies on 6 March 1936, powered by the soon to be equally famous Rolls-Royce Merlin I engine. However, due to production problems encountered with the revolutionary stressed-skin construction of the fighter, it was to be another two-and-a-half years before the first Spitfire Is entered service with Fighter Command.

To many ex-Fighter Command pilots the first production types were the best handling of the breed, being a 'true aviator's aircraft', with beautifully harmonised flying controls - married to a light weight airframe. It was a major leap forward in technology for RAF fighter pilots who had been weaned on a diet of open cockpit biplanes, and it instilled in them the confidence to counter the new breed of Luftwaffe fighter, the deadly Bf 109.

Over the nine years of its production life the Spitfire's basic shape was to alter very little, but under the skin the story was vastly different. As the power output of firstly the Merlin, and then Griffon engines increased, so too did the weight of the fighter.

An indication of this growth can be seen by comparing the maximum speed and loaded weights of the Mk I of 1938 with the F 24 of 1947. The former could achieve 355 mph at an optimum height of 19,000 ft, with a loaded weight of 5819 lbs, whilst the latter had a top speed of 454 mph at 26,000 ft, and was cleared to take-off at a weight of 9900 lbs.

The versatility of the design had also been realised during its long production life, the Packard-Merlin-powered Mk XVI of 1945, for example, being cleared to carry a 500-lb bomb on its centreline, or a single 250-lb device under each wing, or alternatively a battery of unguided rocket projectiles fitted with 60-lb warheads. Indeed, in the last year of the war the Spitfire proved to be more usefully employed by the Allies as a dedicated ground attack aircraft than in its proven day fighter role.

Tackling Bf 109s over the Channel, neutralising V-rocket launch sites in Belgium and Holland or flying high and low-level reconnaissance sorties deep into the Fatherland, the Spitfire was always considered to be a pilot's aircraft by the tens of thousands that flew it in the various theatres of war across the globe. This was achieved by the implementation of a rigorous development phase on the engineering side that kept apace with the increasing demands of war, Vickers-Supermarine ensuring that the aircraft adhered to R J Mitchell's original concept by remaining receptive to the pilot's touch – despite the aforementioned weight growth, power increase and broadening of its operational remit.

▲ No 121 'Eagle' Sqn Spitfire Mk VB at Southend in August 1942

▶ Sqn Ldr A D Farquhar and a Spitfire Mk I of No 602 Sqn at Drem in February 1940

'We were always on the defensive due to the Bf 109E's greater ceiling, and our staple tactic was to turn straight into them so that they couldn't latch onto your tail. You then pulled on the "g" in the hope that your own superior rate of turn would allow you to whip around on to their tails. Often, having performed this manoeuvre on two or three consecutive occasions, you would right yourself only to find the sky empty of friend or foe! Then the search began all over again.'
Flt Sgt George Unwin, No 19 Sqn, Fowlmere, 1940

'I was now all set to renew acquaintances with the formidable Focke-Wulfs, but this time I was better equipped. The Biggin Hill squadrons (Nos 611 and 341 Sqns) were using the Spitfire IXBs (actually officially known as LF IXCs, and fitted with the Merlin 66 engine – squadron pilots referred to this mark as the 'Mk IXB', and christened the F IXC the 'Mk IXA', the latter being powered by a Merlin 61, 63 or 63A engine), a mark of Spitfire markedly superior in performance to the Fw 190A below 27,000 ft. Unlike the Spitfire IXA, with which all other Spitfire IX wings in the Group were equipped, the IXB's supercharger came in at a lower altitude and the aircraft attained its best performance at 21,000 ft, or at roughly the same altitude as the Fw 190. At this height it was approximately 30 mph faster, was better in the climb and vastly more manoeuvrable. As an all-round fighter the Spitfire IXB was supreme, and undoubtedly the best mark of Spitfire produced, despite later and more powerful versions.'

Wg Cdr Al Deere, Wing Leader, Biggin Hill Wing, 1943

▲ Spitfire LF IXC

◀ Spitfire LF IXE

▲ Spitfire PR XIX
◀ Spitfire LF XVIE

◀ Spitfire Mk IA
▶ Spitfire LF IXC

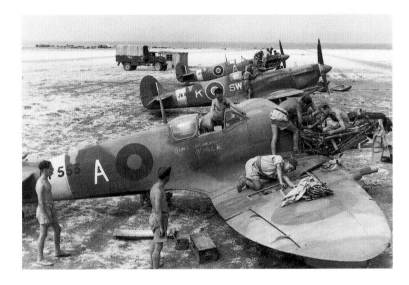

'The new 1600 hp Merlin 61 engine was designed for bombers but it was soon found that it could be housed in an extended Mk V airframe. Individual ejector exhausts were fitted and a four-blade Rotol airscrew absorbed the extra engine power at high altitudes. The supercharger cut in automatically at about 19,000 ft (6000 m), which gave a top speed of about 410 mph (660 km/h). In short, the Spitfire Mk IX was the best fighting aeroplane of its day. Its great tactical advantage was that, apart from its longer nose and more numerous exhaust stacks, it looked exactly like the inferior Spitfire Mk V, and in the air the Germans would not know the difference – until we hit them.'
Wg Cdr Johnnie Johnson, Wing Leader, Tangmere Wing, 1943

▲ Spitfire Mk V trops in Italy in 1944

◄ Spitfire LF XVIE ►

◀ Spitfire LF IXC

▶ Spitfire PR XI

'Flying on Photographic Reconnaissance (PR) was regarded by many pilots, and especially by those fortunate enough to actually do it, as a "plum" job in the wartime RAF. You sat behind a throbbing Merlin 70 engine, powering a waxed and polished blue Spitfire PR XI whose wings had been stripped of guns and ammunition to hold extra gallons of petrol in the leading-edges, as it flew at 360 mph to a target hundreds of miles into enemy airspace to take urgently-needed photographs and, avoiding hostile flak and fighter interception, to return with them to base. This was the stuff of many a young pilot's dreams. . .'

Flt Lt 'Jimmy' Taylor, No 16 Sqn, Northolt, 1944

'On our first patrol, just after dawn, we climbed to our allotted height of 10,000 ft (3000 m), and about ten miles from Dieppe I could see a heavy pall of dark smoke over the town. On the radio some Spitfire leader was ordering his pilots to fight their way out, and another reported more enemy fighters approaching from inland. Ahead of us a mass of aeroplanes milled about the sky. I could see '190s above and my flight commander, Denis Crowley-Milling, called the break. We swung round together to find the '190s at our own level, in pairs and fours. A '190 zoomed from below and appeared ahead of my section of four Spitfires. I gave him a long burst, cannon and machine-guns, from the maximum range. Surprisingly it began to smoke, the wheels dropped and it fell into the sea.'

Sqn Ldr Johnnie Johnson, OC No 610 Sqn, Ludham, 1942

▲ Looking through the Barr and Stroud GM 2 gunsight of a Spitfire Mk I in Aug 1940

◄ Spitfire Mk XI

▶ Spitfire Mk VB

'The two-stage/two-speed supercharger of the Mk 61 Merlin was a revelation in the Mk IX, with the former coming in with a bang at an altitude of about 19,000 ft. One drawback of the new machine, however, was that it could be tipped on its nose more easily, due to the centre of gravity having shifted forward because of the elongated engine nacelle required to house the "blown" Merlin.'

Sqn Ldr Pete Brothers, Supernumerary Wing Leader, Hornchurch Wing, 1942

'The Mk XIV was a hairy beast to fly, and took some getting used too. Fortunately, Madura boasted a concrete runway that was over 3000 yards long, having been an important base for RAF Liberator units bombing Burma and Malaya in 1944/45 – it was just the ticket for a squadron coming to grips for the first time with the vicious torque swing of the Griffon engine. We were told to open the throttle very slowly at the start of our take-off, with full opposite rudder applied to offset the five-bladed prop, which was driven by the Griffon in the opposite direction to the Merlin – this took some getting used to! Even with full aileron, elevator and rudder, this brute of a fighter still took off slightly sideways. However, once you picked up flying speed, and trimmed the rudder and elevator, this torque pull became bearable.

'One aspect you always had to bear in mind with the Mk XIV was that no flying surface trimming could allow for its considerable weight – it tipped the scales at 8475 lbs when fuelled and armed, which made it over 2000 lbs heavier than the Mk VIII. Therefore, extra height had to be allowed for rolls and loops, as it tended to "wash out" when being flown in this way. "Ginger" Lacey graphically demonstrated just how serious a problem this was when he attempted to do a loop from what he thought was an adequate starting height over Madura one afternoon. At the bottom of the loop he cleared the ground by barely four feet, and upon recovering back at the field, looked ten years older when he extricated his sweat-soaked body from the cockpit. He immediately gathered us around and told us in no uncertain terms not to attempt a similar manoeuvre with anything less than a 4000-ft reading on the altimeter.'

Flt Lt Don Healey, No 17 Sqn, Madura, 1945

▲ Spitfire PR XIX of No 2 Sqn at Celle, Germany, in 1947

▶ Spitfire Mk VIII

'I spent an interesting day with Jeffrey Quill at Worthy Down flying a new Spitfire, a Mk XII fitted with a Rolls-Royce Griffon 2000 hp engine. It was quite a machine. If you opened up too quickly, the engine would take charge and you found yourself careering across the airfield at right angles to your intended take-off run. It was really fast at low-level – over 400 mph – and though eventually only two squadrons operated these aircraft, they were more than a match for the low-level Fw 190s which the Germans were using on "tip-and-run" bombing and strafing raids against the south coast towns and military installations. Operating alongside the Typhoons, they could catch the Fw 190s fairly easily. But to me this was the end of the line: engine power had outgrown the airframe. It looked a bit clumsy with its slightly drooping nose, but it was great fun to fly, and in any case the later version – the Mk XIV – with modifications to the airframe and a five-bladed propeller, became a fine combat aircraft.'

Wg Cdr Wilfred Duncan-Smith, Wing Leader, North Weald Wing, 1942

▲ Spitfire LF IXC

▶ Spitfire FR XVIIIE and LF XVIE

▲ Spitfire FR XIVE

◀ Spitfire Mk VB

'Although the Merlin-powered Spitfires were nicer to fly from a handling point of view, the Mk XIV was the real performer thanks to its Griffon engine. It was a truly impressive machine, being able to climb almost vertically – it gave many Luftwaffe fighter pilot the shock of their lives when, having thought they had bounced you from a superior height, they were astonished to find the Mk XIV climbing up to take them on head-on, throttle wide open!'
Wg Cdr Pete Brothers, Wing Leader, Culmhead Wing, 1944

▲ Spitfire LF XVIE

▶ Spitfire PR XI seen in July 1944

◀ Spitfire LF IXE

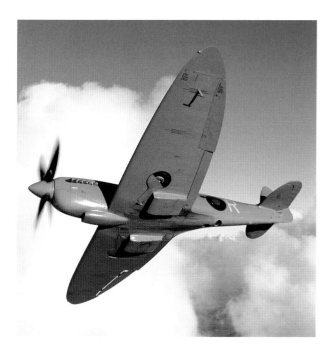

'In June we were the first fighter wing to move into Normandy, which meant that we could range deeper over France in search of the Luftwaffe. The enemy was now beginning to appear in large formations. On one of these occasions we bounced a gaggle over the River Seine, and I soon got a brace of Fw 190s, the second at low-level. I was alone and since there were a lot of German fighters milling about, I cautiously began to regain height, keeping a very sharp look-out and clearing my tail every few seconds. At 4300 m (14,000 ft) I thought I saw six Spitfires, slightly above. I called whom I thought to be the leader, and told him that I was just ahead of him and to form-up to me. I learned of my stupid error when the leader of the six Messerschmitts opened fire, and during the subsequent fight – one of the hardest – my Spitfire took a cannon shell in the wing root. Eventually, I managed to throw them off, and on returning found we had destroyed twelve for the loss of three Canadians.'

**Wg Cdr Johnnie Johnson, Wing Leader,
Canadian Wing, Normandy, 1944**

◀ Spitfire LF IXC   ▲ Spitfire PR XI   ▶ Spitfire LF IXC & PR XI

▲ Spitfire FR XVIIIE ▶

Bristol

BLENHEIM

'As one slid down through the roof hatch into the small, cluttered, cockpit, the big Mercury engines obstructed much of the sideways view and all of the wings. The nose was short and fell away rapidly. The general impression for the pilot was that the Blenheim was just two big engines stuck at the end of the wing root.' **Flg Off 'Dopey' Edwards, No 233 Sqn, Leuchars, 1939**

Unlike most of its frontline contemporaries serving in the RAF at the time of the declaration of war, Bristol's venerable Blenheim was the result of a speculative private venture on the part of the manufacturers, rather than a design built to a specific Air Ministry request. Unencumbered by restrictions on the aircraft's weight, powerplants, general layout or radius of action, the Bristol design team, led by Frank Barnwell, produced drawings and models for a sleek twin-engined machine known as the Type 142. In an unprecedented step, the actual 'green light' was given to the project not by the RAF or the Air Ministry, but by newspaper magnate, Lord Rothermere, who, in 1934, approached Bristol with a desire to obtain a fast, medium-sized, transport for his own use. In order to meet the Lord's stringent speed requirements, the Type 142's Bristol Aquila engines of 500 hp were replaced by a pair of Bristol Mercury VISs of 650 hp apiece.

First flown at Filton on 12 April 1935, the aircraft's performance sent ripples through the RAF when it was discovered that the transport's top speed was a full 30 mph greater than Gloster Gauntlet I fighter, which had just entered service with the air force. The Air Ministry approached Lord Rothermere in the hope of being able to borrow the aircraft in order to test its possible military applications, but its owner went one step better by presenting the Type 142, by now christened *Britain First*, to the nation. Bristol had also quickly realised the offensive potential of the design also, and hurriedly produced the Type 142M which, in the summer of 1935, the Air Ministry ordered as Specification 28/35 to the tune of 150 airframes.

Christened the Blenheim, the first Mk Is entered service with No 114 Sqn in March 1937. The unit was soon grabbing the headlines thanks to their high speed runs at that year's Hendon Pageant, the last of its type ever staged.

These public performances, allied with the results of exercise staged against Fighter Command's predominantly biplane-equipped squadrons, led many to believe that the Blenheim was the world's most formidable bomber, and production orders for the Mk I soared to a staggering 1552 airframes. By September 1939, most UK-based Blenheim squadrons had replaced their Mk Is with the improved Mk IV, the latter having grown out of an Air Ministry requirement for a general recce type with greater crew accommodation and an increased range. Initially, the first Mk IVs had been built under licence in Canada as the Bolingbroke I, and the modified Blenheim was slowly introduced to British production lines towards the end of 1938 – No 90 Sqn debuted the Mk IV to frontline service in March 1939.

As the backbone type in Bomber Command at the start of hostilities, it fell to the Mk IV to make both the first recce incursion into German airspace (on 3 September 1939) and to drop bombs on German targets (24 hours later). Ominously for the crews taking part, two of the ten bombers despatched were shot down. Over the next three years Blenheim crews first struggled to stem the *Blitzkrieg* in the Low Countries, and then attempted to take the war to occupied Europe from 'Fortress Britain' in the first Channel sweeps, which resulted in alarming losses. Overseas the story was little better, as Blenheims fell like flies to Axis fighters in the Middle East, Mediterranean and the Far East.

The Blenheim was also pressed into service by Fighter Command, modified aircraft boasting four Browning guns in a pack beneath the fuselage. Designated the Mk IF, the type enjoyed little success during daylight hours, but was soon modified into a promising nightfighter when paired with the first airborne radar sets. The Mk IVF continued on in this role through the night blitz of 1940/41.

▲ Blenheim Mk IV V6083 of No 13 Operational Training Unit in 1942

▶ Blenheim Mk IFs of No 604(F) Sqn during Air Defence Exercises held in July 1939

'After I had been in the squadron for about three months I was at last checked out on the new Blenheims with which 29 was being re-equipped. Previously I had been content with flying the Demons or going up as a passenger in a Blenheim with one of the older members of the unit. We had heard a lot of nasty stories about the Blenheim from visiting bomber boys. One such story was that if you couldn't get the undercarriage down and had to belly-land, the aircraft would go up in flames. Nevertheless, I had no trouble with my check-out. From then on I got my fair share of squadron flying, and was an accepted member of the 29th.'

Plt off Bob Braham, No 29 Sqn, Debden, 1939

▲ Blenheim Is near completion in the Bristol factory in March 1939

▶ Blenheim Mk IVF

'Fleet Street started a daily "scorecard", giving details of "runs made", "hits scored", "aircraft – friends and opposition – "knocked down" and a "summary" of the day's play. "Blenheims versus Stavanger" was the headline – what else did they have for the front pages? But on the 9th of May we returned to Wattisham for a rest – "retired hurt"!'

Sgt Len Fearnley, No 107 Sqn, Wattisham, 1940

◀ Blenheim Mk IVF ▶

▼ Blenheim Mk Is of No 90 Sqn at Bicester on Armistice Day 1938

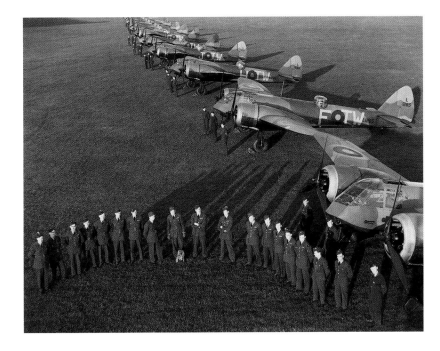

'Talk of the Phoney War in the British Press sounded pretty sour to us – it was anything but phoney – and the "remounts" coming out from Andover were very skimpily trained: 10 to 12 hours on Blenheims. One was reminded of the First World War "at the front", and we'd only just started this one! The onset of one of the severest winters for years all but stopped flying. Poorly maintained French roads started to crumble, and on the Rosières airfield a complete First War trench system opened up which added to the interest of take-off and landing. We re-equipped with Mk IV Blenheims during the winter, which provided a few welcome days home on ferrying trips. I think most of us preferred flying the Bristol-built Is to the "shadow" factory IVs, although the latter had 9-lb boost, long-range tanks, and better navigational facilities.'

Flt Lt G M Wyatt, No 57 Sqn, Rosières-en-Santerre, 1939

'It seemed to take an age for the range to close but it must have been only a few minutes. Not only was I excited but I opened fire at too great a range, and unpardonably without identifying the aircraft. My tracers showed that I was too far out, so I continued to close more coolly. Now I recognised it as a Dornier twin-engined bomber. Other searchlights were sweeping the sky near us and, as I continued to close the range, I caught a brief glimpse of a Hurricane diving through a searchlight beam. He was above me and suddenly I heard Wilsden's gun rattling away in the back. I realised that he must be shooting at the Hurricane in error, as the Dornier was still ahead of us. I shouted over the intercom to him to cease fire, but too late as I could see in the light of the searchlights that the Hurricane was streaming what looked like glycol from its engine.'

Plt Off Bob Braham, No 29 Sqn, Debden, 1940

▲ Blenheim Mk IVF ▶

Curtiss
P-40 KITTYHAWK

'We had a steady airplane in the P-40. We had better armament and we had an instructor in General Chennault who knew how to take advantage of the P-40's strength.' **Maj John Alison, 23rd FG, China, 1942**

Overshadowed by other more successful USAAF fighter types like the P-38, P-47 and P-51, the Curtiss P-40 was nevertheless the primary Army Air Force fighter at the time of the Japanese fleet's surprise attack on Pearl Harbor on 7 December 1941. Along with smaller numbers of the obsolescent Curtiss P-36 and Bell P-39 Airacobra, the P-40 was responsible for 'holding the line' in the Pacific for much of 1942, vainly attempting to blunt the aerial onslaught unleashed by the Japanese Army and Navy Air Forces.

The last in a long line of fighters to carry the appellation 'Hawk', the P-40 family was born out of the marriage of an early-production P-36A fuselage with the all-new Allison V-1710-19 turbosupercharged and liquid-cooled inline engine. When first flown on 14 October 1938 as the Hawk 81, Curtiss engineers could never have imagined that roughly 13,800 aircraft, in a handful of sub-types, would be built between early 1939 and December 1944, and used in virtually every theatre of conflict during World War 2. The first inkling of the success that lay ahead for the design came however, with the US Army's initial order for 524 airframes (the largest single order for a combat type up to that point), which was placed just six months after the prototype's first flight.

These aircraft lacked many of the standard features associated with comparable European fighters of the day – cockpit armour, self-sealing tanks and a substantial armament – although few saw combat in the European theatre when hostilities commenced. A batch destined for the French Air Force wound up with the RAF following the French capitulation. Curtiss redressed the initial 'survivability' shortcomings with the service debut of the P-40B and C models in mid-1941, although the additional weight of the aforementioned vital combat equipment had a negative effect on the performance.

However, the P-40 went on to become *the* fighter for low altitude theatres such as North Africa and China. The aircraft's performance below 12,000 ft was comparable, if not superior to the axis aircraft it was engaging in these arenas. The dive capabilities of the P-40 were legendary and, tied in with one of the best pairs of ailerons 'in the business', this meant that the P-40 was held in high regard by its aircrews, who were flying in some of the toughest conditions of the war.

It was in these latter conflicts that the aircraft perhaps enjoyed its greatest moments of glory. For example, in China, 90 Hawk 81A-3s from a British order were diverted to Maj-Gen Claire Chennault's American Volunteer Group (AVG) in China – a mercenary band of pilots who were almost single-handedly attempting to combat the overwhelming Japanese bombing raids on Chinese strategic points. Fighting both the enemy and a constant shortage of spare parts, the 'Flying Tigers', as they were soon dubbed, were credited with the destruction of 286 Japanese aircraft for the loss of just 23 American pilots.

The basic P-40 airframe remained essentially unchanged throughout its production life and the Allison engine was continually improved from 930 hp to 1425 hp but with the single stage 'blower' the critical altitude was always around 12, 000 ft.

The final production P-40 built (to the tune of no less than 4219 examples) was the N-model, which combined a drastically lightened fuselage and the ever-reliable V-1710-81 engine of 1200 hp. Although this tried and tested combination was inferior to virtually all other Axis fighters by late 1943, the P-40N continued to perform sterling work in the demanding ground attack role until war's end, its durability and crisp handling making it a favourite with pilots from the RAF, USAAF, Soviet Air Forces, RNZAF and RAAF, to name

▲ P-40Fs take-off from El Kabrit in March 1943

▶ Desert Air Force Kittyhawk Mk IIIs taxy out in North Africa in November 1943

'He had a Hurricane; fortunately it was one of the eight-gun Hurricanes, which was just about equal with the P-40. I not only held my own against this British ace (I think he had 21 victories), I was able to get on his tail and he was quite surprised. But I was fighting where he was at a disadvantage at 3000 ft. We fought at this altitude so the group below could see us. The P-40 was a low-altitude airplane. The Hurricane was a high-altitude airplane to get the German bombers, so it did not perform well at low altitudes. At a higher altitude I'm sure he would have been able to take me easily. He landed and came up to me and said, "I thought you Yanks were just all mouth". Then he added, "You did very well."'

Capt John Alison, Britain, 1941

▲ Tomahawk Mk I and No. 87 Sqn Hurricane I, RAF Colerne Feb 6 1941

▶ Kittyhawk Mk I

'Our P-40s were faster than the Nakajima I-97s they flew, and after we had spread out the enemy, we learned to whack them off one by one. Our P-40 proved to be capable of taking a beating from gunfire and yet go on flying. No longer did we turn with the Japs when we didn't have to; we made them play our game.'

Lt Gregory 'Pappy' Boyington, First Pursuit Squadron, American Volunteer Group, Mingaladon Field, 1942

▲ Kittyhawk Mk I

▶ With its nose smeared in oil from a recently downed Zero, P-40E *Scatter Brain* of the 49th FG is rearmed at Dobodura, New Guinea, in May 1943

◀ P-40K

▼ Kittyhawk Mk I ▶

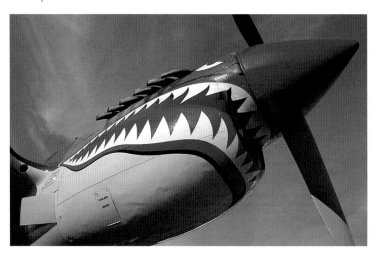

'The P-40 could out-dive just about anything, and indicated airspeeds near 600 mph were not unheard of. However, it did want to pull to the right in a dive, and when it was desirable to hold it straight, as for dive-bombing, it needed a lot of left rudder pressure – so much so it was alleged that one could always spot a P-40 pilot by the over-developed muscles in his left leg!'

Lt William Stubbs, Ninth Air Force, North Africa, 1943

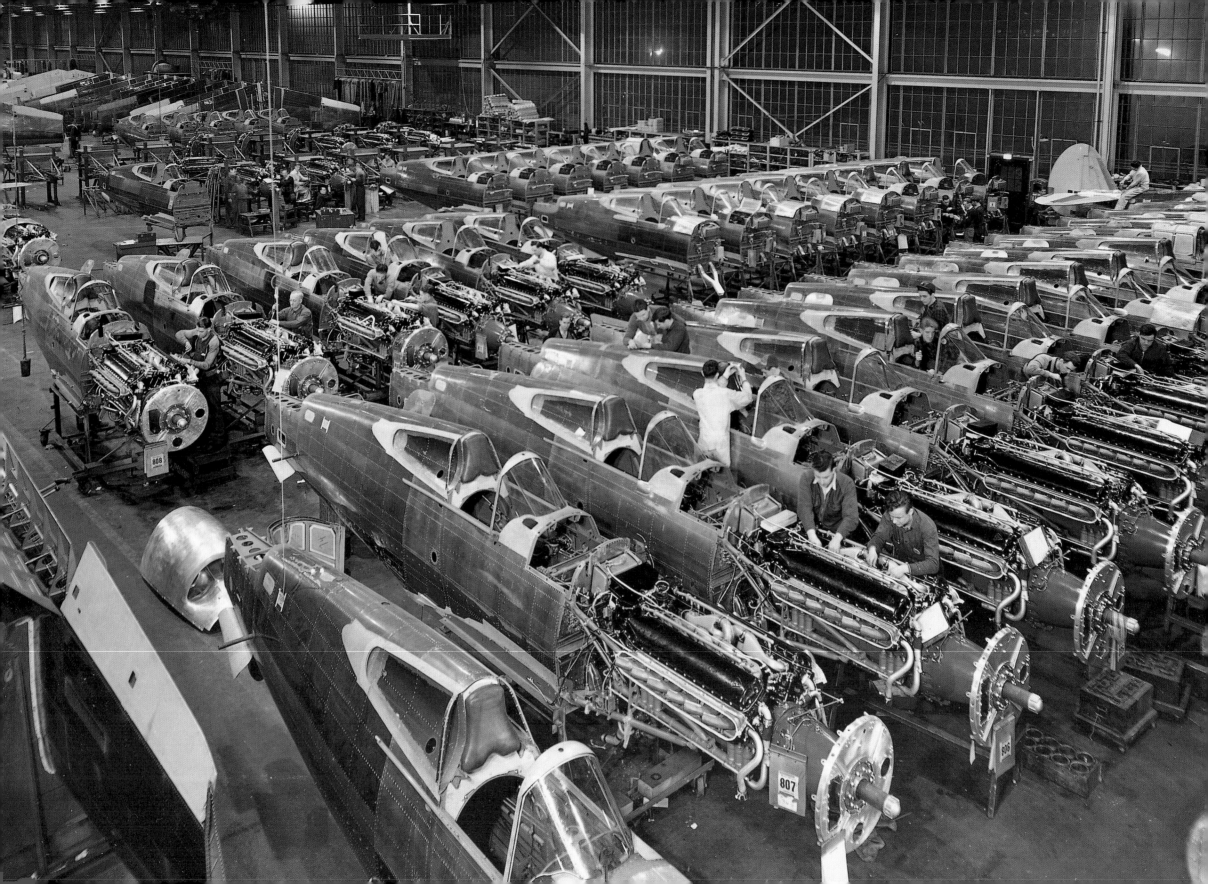

◀ Curtiss-Wright Airplane Division at Buffalo churns out P-40Es in 1941

▶ Kittyhawk Mk I

'An AVG pilot, apparently feeling no pain from good Scotch, said "The Japs can out-turn you. But no one, no one, can follow a P-40 when it dives". This statement turned out to be very true, for it was not until the Messerschmitt 109E came along that a P-40 pilot couldn't dive away when he so chose. The slow-climbing P-40 used this evasive manoeuvre until an Me 109E pilot sportingly displayed what his new plane could do in North Africa when they first came out with the 109. As the firsthand story was told to me, the South African pilot had dived out, pointing his P-40 straight down, but, much to his amazement, a German Me 109E pilot slowly passed him in his dive, holding up the first two fingers of his left hand in a "V" for victory!'

Lt Gregory 'Pappy' Boyington, First Pursuit Squadron, American Volunteer Group, Mingaladon Field, 1942

'The air was so full of planes it reminded me of a cadet centre. My section and I drew blood with our first bursts as I saw three of the oncoming aircraft pull away leaving heavy smoke trails indicating they had run into our concentrated fire. I'm afraid it was an even trade as I could hear the metallic "clink" when several rounds from the enemies' guns entered my fuselage in the nose section. A second or two later I became aware of the definite odour of my coolant, and correctly judged that I had been hit in the glycol tank. I spun down out of the fight and as I recovered from the spin I saw an American plane under attack by one of the enemy. I dived on the Messerschmitt, gave him one long burst from my machine-guns, and saw my tracers entering his fuselage at the wing root. The German half-rolled and plunged into the sea in the inverted position.'

Maj Archie Knight, 57th FG, Tunisia, 1943

▲ Kittyhawk Mk I
◄ P-40M

'Pulling the nose up slightly, I observed the tracers strike the aircraft from end to end. Heavy black smoke and then flames started to come from the engine and the Zeke dropped off on one wing, headed for the ground. By then another Zero had caught up with me and I was forced to dive to lose him. My prop was indicating 4000 rpms when the nose section of my P-40 exploded and the engine caught fire. I cut off the switches and was prepared to jump when the fire went out. Off to the left I noticed a large kunai field and I was able to crash-land the P-40 without too much trouble.'
Lt Joel Thorvaldson, 49th FG, Dobodura, 1943

▲ Kittyhawk Mk IIIs of No 260 Sqn in the Western Desert in 1942

◀ Kittyhawk Mk I

▶ P-40K

Grumman
F4F WILDCAT

'The Martlet/Wildcat really was ideally suited to carrier aviation, and I've yet to meet an ex-F4F/FM-2 pilot who has anything bad to say about the aircraft.' **Capt Eric 'Winkle' Brown, 1994**

Derived from a biplane design offered in competition to the more modern Brewster F2A Buffalo monoplane, the Wildcat was the result of a study undertaken by Grumman into the feasibility of a single wing naval fighter. The company had been a major supplier of carrier-based aircraft in the 1930s, and with other manufacturers turning to monoplane designs both in the US and abroad, it was logical that any new Grumman design should follow suit. The XF4F-1 biplane layout was therefore modified on the drawing board in early 1936, and following appraisal by the Navy, a prototype was approved for building. Designated the XF4F-2, the fighter took to the skies for the first time on 2 September 1937, powered by a 1050 hp Pratt & Whitney Twin Wasp radial engine.

Despite being faster than the rival Brewster, the XF4F-2 lost out in the fly-off against the Buffalo due to the latter's superior handling qualities, but Grumman was encouraged enough by the US Navy to drastically rework its prototype into the vastly superior XF4F-3 of March 1939. A more powerful Twin Wasp engine with a two-stage supercharger was

fitted, wing span and area increased, the tail surfaces redesigned and an improved armament installed. After flight trials, the Navy immediately ordered 78 production F4F-3s, which they christened the Wildcat.

The type also solicited interest from European customers in the form of France and Greece, who were trying to rearm in response to aggressive overtures emanating from Germany. Neither country received their Wildcats before invasion, however, and the Royal Navy in turn acquired these surplus fighters, which were technically far in advance of anything they were then operating. On the other side of the Atlantic, the first F4F-3s to enter US Navy service were delivered to VF-7 at the end of 1940, and within six months half a dozen Navy and Marine Corps squadrons were operating their full quota of Wildcats. The -3 was superseded by the -4 in the autumn of 1941, this improved fighter embodying improvements recommended by the British following combat in their Martlet Is.

US Navy/Marine Corps Wildcats fired their guns in anger for the first time immediately after the Pearl Harbor raid when a handful of VMF-211 F4F-3s attempted to blunt an overwhelming force of Japanese carrier aircraft during the assault on Wake Island. Although defeated on this occasion, the Wildcat went on to acquit itself well during the 'dark days' of 1942/43 in the great carrier battles at Coral Sea and Midway – it also played a starring role in the assault on Guadalcanal.

In April 1942 General Motors' Eastern Aircraft Division was awarded a contract to build F4F-4s, which they duly designated FM-1s. In late 1943 GM switched production to the FM-2, which was based on Grumman's XF4F-8, the improved fighter differing from its predecessor principally in respect to its powerplant – the turbocharged Wright R-1820-56 Cyclone had replaced the now venerable Twin Wasp. This swap made for a higher top speed and an optimum altitude some 50 per cent greater than that achieved in the FM-1. A taller fin and rudder was also built into the FM-2 to help maintain directional stability in light of the increased horsepower 'up front'. By the time production was terminated in August 1945, no less than 4777 FM Wildcats had been built.

◀ Martlet IVs of No 893 Sqn run up prior to launching from HMS *Formidable* in the Mediterranean in February 1943

▶ F4F-4s of an anonymous US Navy training unit seen in October 1943

'I was in a great position above and to the right of the leader's wingman, so I shot him in the engine and wingroot with a burst long enough to cause him to flame and explode. That either surprised or made the Zero lead really mad, because he did the tightest turn I've ever seen to try to get on me. But I also pulled up into a tight climbing left turn into him, and he missed his shot behind me. The FM-2's tight turn must have surprised him because I got around quickly on him into a head-on, and put a fast burst into his engine. That really made him mad, because he quickly pulled hard up into me in what I thought was an attempt to ram. I had also pulled up hard to avoid him – it was a close thing. The Zero leader was flying a dark-green aircraft with no white circles around the "red meatballs", and he had large white letters and numbers on his tail, with what looked like a white streak of lightning or slash marking across his tail below the letters and numbers. I had the feeling he was an old hand, and expected the old Wildcat to be easy prey, so he was surprised and let his temper get the better of him – he probably didn't know about the much-improved FM-2.'

Ens Joseph McGraw, VC-80, USS Manila Bay, *1944*

▲ F4F-4s of VF-11 'Sundowners' lined up at Henderson Field, on Guadalcanal, in May 1943

▶ F4F-3 Wildcat

'On this particular morning, for VF-6's second flight we got no warning, just "Pilots, man your planes". Flight quarters were sounded on the PA system, followed immediately by "Pilots, man your planes". What the hell was going on? We ran to our ready room and grabbed navigation boards – we had no idea where we were going or what the mission was. I manned my plane, which was already turning up. That had never happened before. Nobody started my F4F except me! The young plane captain, about 18 years old, said "Mr Daniels, they told me to start the airplane. They told me!" I said "All right, don't worry about it. Is it all right?" He said "Yes, Sir, the plane checks out". We had no time to really warm up our engines. As we taxied into position, one of the plane handlers held up a little blackboard. On it was written: "Japs attack Pearl Harbor. No shit."'

Ens Jim Daniels, VF-6, USS Enterprise, *1941*

▲ FM-2 Wildcat

◄ Martlet I AL257 is marshalled out for a training flight in April 1941

'The F4F-4 mounted a solid battery of six .50-calibre machine-guns, three in each wing, and sported a good reflector sight. On the down side, the airplane was moderately underpowered, and therefore quite slow in the climb, a compromise necessitated by the wing-folding mechanism, heavy armoured seatbacks and heavy ammunition load required for the six machine guns. About the best thing that could be said about the added weight was that it would help Wildcats get away from most Japanese and German fighters while in a dive. Already proven at Coral Sea and Midway, the Wildcat had a reputation for standing up to heavy fire and bringing its pilot home. While no thoroughbred, the Wildcat was still the best, most powerful, most reliable production fighter the Navy had thus far put into service. I, for one, was glad to have it.'

Lt Cdr Tommy Blackburn, VGF-29, NAS Norfolk, 1942

▲ Fleet Air Arm pilot prepares for a mission

◀ FM-2 Wildcat

▶ F4F-3 Wildcat

Westland
LYSANDER

'The "Lizzie" had the look of a dragonfly about it, because of its long and slender wings seemingly about to part company with the tubby fuselage hanging underneath. People who were useless at aircraft recognition used to divide up flying machines into two groups – aeroplanes and Lysanders.' **Bill Gunston, aviation historian**

The first purpose-built army co-operation aircraft to enter service with the RAF, the Westland Lysander filled a role previously performed by modified bomber types like its immediate predecessor, the Hawker Hector. Constructed to Air Ministry Specification A39/34, the first prototype, designated P.8 by Westlands, made its maiden flight on 15 June 1936. Following a short series of handling sorties, minor modifications were carried out before the prototype was cleared to perform at the SBAC event at Hatfield (the pre-war equivalent of the Farnborough airshow) later in June – these changes were essentially the only revisions made by Westlands to their original prototype prior to series production commencing in 1937.

The Air Ministry had placed an order for 144 Lysanders in September 1936, and the first unit to re-equip with the aircraft was No 16 Sqn at Old Sarum in June 1938 – this dedicated army co-operation squadron had previously flown the Hawker Audax since 1933. By 1939 production had got into full swing, and the RAF took delivery of 66 airframes, with No 16 Sqn bringing its strength up to 14 aircraft. By the outbreak of war seven units had fully re-equipped with the Lysander, allowing the Hector to be consigned to second-line tasks. Most of the home-based 'Lizzie' units were by now operating the Mk II version of the aircraft, which boasted a 905 hp Bristol Perseus XII in place of the original 890 hp unit. No less than 442 Mk IIs were built during the early years of the war, and the type was the first to see action in France with the British Expeditionary Force (BEF) in May 1940 following the ending of the Phoney War. Four squadrons had been sent to France early in the New Year, and once hostilities started, the true vulnerability of the type came to the fore – 11 Lysanders were lost between 10 and 23 May, and this was just the start.

Capable of barely 200 mph, and tasked with flying in unfriendly skies dominated by enemy fighters of the calibre of the Bf 109E and Bf 110, the Lysander crews had to rely on the aircraft's superb manoeuvrability at low-level in order to successfully carry out their mission. During the course of the bitter fighting over Belgium and northern France, a

number of crews succeeded in shooting down a variety of German types including Messerschmitt fighters and a Ju 87! However, these victories were very much the exception to the rule, and in total some 118 aircraft and 120 aircrew were lost during the doomed campaign in France.

The Lysander was quickly relegated to second-line duties in the aftermath of the BEF disaster, the RAF being forced to revise their army co-op theories. Ironically, it was whilst performing tasks that had never previously been thought of for the Lysander that the type really came into its own. Its role with the clandestine Special Duties squadrons is the stuff of legend, the aircraft proving ideal for performing supply drops and transporting agents into and out of occupied Europe under the cover of darkness – the type's proven short-field performance was the key to the Lysander's success. The aircraft also proved useful in the air-sea rescue role over the Channel, a small number of specialised Coastal Command squadrons being equipped with suitably-modified Lysanders (dinghies and supplies bolted onto the wheel sponson racks) at key Fighter Command bases along the coast.

▲ Lysander Mk Is await collection by the RAF from Westland's Yeovil factory in March 1939

▶ Attack! A trio of No 4 Sqn Lysander Mk IIs dive at a target during exercises in France in early spring 1940

'The original army co-operation requirements demanded not only an exceptional small-field performance, but a good all-round view for the pilot. In fact, the outlook from the driver's seat was probably better than in any other single piston-engined military aircraft produced before or since. The pilot sat high up, as if on a dais, looking over the top of the engine cowling. He could see sideways and downwards through deep windows which could be slid down almost to seat level, and upwards through a transparent roof which extended aft between the thin-section, narrow-chord, inner-wing section. For an ex-amateur turned ferry pilot like myself, who was learning this new trade in the first months of the war, the delivery of a Lysander was a nearly ideal assignment.'

Flg Off H A Taylor, No 9 Maintenance Unit, Cosford, 1940

▲ Lysander Mk IIIA ▶

◀ Lysander Mk IIIA ▶

▼ Marvellously posed 'action' shot of a Lysander Mk II pilot checking grid references with his colleagues in the Scots Guards during a combined RAF/Army exercise staged in October 1941

'The Lysander might fairly be described as an interestingly schizophrenic affair. When treated like a normal aeroplane it behaved more or less as such – when required by short-field circumstances or at the whim of a test pilot, to provide a passable imitation of an Autogiro, it became an entirely different and even, if not handled firmly, occasionally recalcitrant device.'

Flg Off H A Taylor, No 9 Maintenance Unit, Cosford, 1940

North American Aviation
B-25 MITCHELL

'A nice sunshiny day with an overcast of anti-aircraft fire.'
Sgt Eldred Scott, 'Doolittle's Raiders', USS Hornet, 1942

Built in response to a pre-war US Army Air Corps proposal for a twin-engined attack bomber, by a company with no previous experience of twin-engined aircraft, bombers or high performance machinery, North American Aviation's B-25 Mitchell proved to be one of the most venerable, and versatile, combat aircraft to see action in World War 2 – indeed, arguably *the* 'bombing twin' of the entire conflict on either side. Built in response to the US Army Air Corps' Circular Proposal 38-385, the prototype (christened the NA-40 by the company) first flew in January 1939, powered by two 1100 hp Pratt & Whitney R-1830 radials. Despite carrying out successful flight trials, NAA were encouraged to

further improve their design by the Army, who now stated that any future medium bomber would have to carry a payload of 2400 lbs – twice that originally stipulated in 38-385.

Re-engineered, and considerably enlarged, the definitive production airframe was designated the NA-62 by NAA and test flown for the first time in September 1939. To offset the detrimental effects of both increasing the all up weight of the airframe and doubling its bombload, company engineers replaced the Pratt & Whitneys with 1300 hp Wright CR-2600 Cyclone engines – this powerplant had already been trialled on the prototype NA-40 several months earlier. So impressed with what they saw on the NAA drawing board, and mindful of the increasing tension in both Europe and Asia, the Army ordered 184 aircraft (to be designated the B-25) before the revised design had even flown.

The first production standard aircraft was flown on 19 August 1940, and was duly christened the Mitchell, after maverick Army bomber proponent, William 'Billy' Mitchell. Like a number of other US Army types then entering service, the B-25 benefited from the lessons being bitterly learnt by the combatants over Europe, and crew armour plating and self-sealing tanks were quickly fitted into production machines by NAA – these aircraft were designated B-25As. Forty A-models were built, and the type saw early combat in World War 2 when an example from the 17th Bombardment Group (Medium) sunk a Japanese submarine off the west coast of mainland America on Christmas Eve 1941. Soon after, a number of B-25Bs were despatched to Australia to help bolster the Allied defence of the island nation. The Mitchell went on to fight not only with the USAAF in the Pacific, but also with US Navy/Marine Corps, British, Dutch and Australian units.

Across the globe, the B-25 was debuted over occupied Europe by No 2 Group, RAF, who used it to replace earlier American 'twins' like the Ventura and Boston. The USAAF medium bomber groups in the ETO and MTO also utilised hundreds of B-25s, and by war's end, the veteran Mitchell was still in production, having outlasted its rivals from Douglas and Martin to become the most prolific American medium bomber of the conflict – built to the tune of 9889 airframes.

◀ An aggressively-marked B-25H seen in the Pacific in 1944

▶ Mitchell II of No 320 Sqn at Dunsfold in April 1944

'The hairiest time of the entire mission probably was the five minutes when they were wheeling our planes into line. Then the actual take-off was scary as the Hornet *was taking green water over the flight deck. I just got myself into the turret – and kept the turret facing aft. I didn't want to watch the take-off, but we made it with feet to spare, which surprised everyone.'*

Sgt David Pohl, 'Doolittle's Raiders', USS Hornet, *1942*

'A group of Russian aviators barged into McChord one night, and they loved the B-25 as much as we did. A Russian General, an interpreter and I got into the plane. The General asked us – or told us – that he was going to take the controls just after we got off the ground. He wasn't kidding. He took us for a ride I'll never forget. When we were just a few feet off the ground he banked the ship and laid it over at a 90-degree angle. I was a passenger standing up, but with the side window just in front of my face. The General insisted on staying right over the city of Washington, and not very high, while he gave the B-25 a test that would frighten a test pilot. He was a wild man, that General, but one hell of a flier.'

Capt Ted Lawson, 'Doolittle's Raiders', McChord Field, 1942

▲ No 98 Sqn Mitchell II seen over Dunsfold in 1944

◀ B-25D Mitchell

▲ B-25J Mitchell ▶

▲ Mitchell IIIs of No 98 Sqn at B58/Melsbroek, in Belgium, in late 1944

◄ B-25D Mitchell

► B-25H Mitchell

North American Aviation
P-51 MUSTANG

'General Kepner (of the Eighth Air Force) got us our P-51s, and within 24 hours of their arrival we were on our first mission. Most people have about 200 hours in a frontline fighter before taking it into combat, We had about 30 minutes!' **Maj Jim Goodson, 4th FG, Debden, 1943**

Arguably the best looking American fighter of World War 2, the P-51 Mustang was also one of a small number of combat aircraft to be conceived, developed and cleared for full-scale production within the six years of world conflict. The Mustang has its origins in a British Purchasing Commission deal struck with North American Aviation (NAA) in April 1940 for an advanced long range fighter. With the RAF standing alone in the face of the impending Luftwaffe onslaught, the agreement stipulated that NAA had to have a completed prototype – tailored to the British specifications – ready for flight within 120 days of the original submission.

Fortunately, the company had already made a start independently of the British deal, with head designers Raymond Rice and Edgar Schmued having engineered their NA-73X to incorporate some of the lessons gleaned from aerial combat in Europe. Three days short of the required date the airframe was completed, but delays with the 1100 hp Allison V-1710-39 engine meant that the prototype did not fly until 26 October 1940. Testing soon bore out the virtues of the design, and the RAF took charge of its first production example in November of the following year. The aircraft handled beautifully and was fast, thanks principally to its revolutionary semi-laminar flow airfoil wing. The British named it the 'Mustang I'.

Like the earlier P-40, which was also powered by the reliable Allison V-1710 engine, the Mustang I soon 'ran out of steam' above 12,000 ft due to its powerplant lacking a two-stage/two-speed supercharger. By that stage in the war, fighter combat was taking place at ceilings well in excess of 20,000 ft where the 'thin' air starved a conventionally aspirated engine, so the Mustang I was fitted with cameras and relegated to the low-level tactical reconnaissance and army co-operation roles.

The USAAF also realised that the Mustang was not good as a fighter above medium altitude and ordered a small number of A-36As and P-51As for ground attack tasks. There the story would have ended had it not been for the RAF sending six Mustang Is to Rolls-Royce for fitting with supercharged Merlin 61 and 65 engines. Once mated with this battle-proven powerplant, the aircraft's performance was startling – a communiqué of the findings was immediately sent to NAA in the US, and the rest is history. The Merlin-powered P-51B made its combat debut over Europe in December 1943, just when the USAAF's much-vaunted daylight bomber campaign had begun to falter due to incredible losses. Here was their 'knight in shinning armour', capable of escorting B-17s and B-24s throughout their hazardous missions.

Over the next 19 months of war in Europe, the Mustang steadily became the dominant USAAF fighter. The RAF, too, got their hands on well over 1000 Merlin-powered aircraft through lend-lease arrangements. In total over 14,819 P-51s were built by North American, plus a further 200 under-licence in Australia. It continued to serve in a frontline capacity with the USAF into the early 1950s, and further afield in Central and South America until the 1970s.

▲ P-51D of the 374th FS/361st FG, based at Bottisham, in mid-1944

▶ Mustang Mk Is of No 2 Sqn at Sawbridgeworth in July 1942

'You've got a horse and a half here m'boy...'
Major Leonard "Kit" Carson, 357th FG

▲ P-51D of the 361st FG over France in 1944

◄ P-51D Mustang ▶

'The weather was sunny, not a cloud in the sky. As we approached the French coast, the sky was full of fighters in one massive dogfight from sea level to the contrail level. In hurried glances, I counted seven parachutes in the air at one time. A couple of miles short of landfall I spotted four Fw 190s off to our right at about 1500ft. Their course and speed was going to put them directly overhead when we crossed the beach. I called Freddie twice with a "tally ho" but there was no response. He did not hear the warnings and apparently did not see the Fw 190s. When Freddie turned left under the enemy to intersect our target road, I tried to radio a warning to him again, but got no response. Once over our target, Freddie turned right for Abbeville, which put us in an ideal position for the Fws to attack. I swung very wide to Freddie's left during the turn, dusting the Abbeville chimney tops. That kept me beneath the Fws, and I believe they lost sight of me.

My plan was to cut off the lead Fw 190 before he could open fire on Freddie, but my timing went to pot when a crashing Spitfire forced me to turn to avoid a collision. That gave the lead Fw pilot time to get into a firing position and he hit Freddie's Mustang with the first burst. I got a long range shot at the Fw leader but he had to break right when his number two man had a go at me. Number two missed and made a big mistake of sliding to my left side ahead of me. It was an easy shot and I hit him hard. His engine caught fire, and soon after it started smoking the canopy came off. I hit him again and he was a goner, falling off to the right into the trees.'

First ever victory credited to a P-51 Mustang –
Flg Off Hollis Hills, No 414 Sqn, Gatwick, 1942

◀ P-51D Mustang

▶ P-51A Mustang wearing the colours of Flg Off Hills aircraft

▲ P-51D Mustang ▶

'The Mustangs, generally speaking, could take harder turns than the people who flew them. Long before the wings flew off the pilot would simply lose consciousness. The blood drained from his head by centrifugal force, measured in Gs. Five Gs and you might "grey out" but be able to function. Six or so and you could "black out" and lose consciousness. With the adoption of G-suits we could cope with these stresses, thus allowing you to fly a little harder and turn a little tighter. We could pull maybe one extra G now, which gave us an edge. There was no resistance to wearing them as we understood what they meant right away – wearing one was the same as making the aeroplane better.'
Capt Clarence 'Bud' Anderson, 357th FG, Leiston, 1944

▲ P-51B 336th FS/4th FG at Debden in 1944

▶ P-51D Mustang

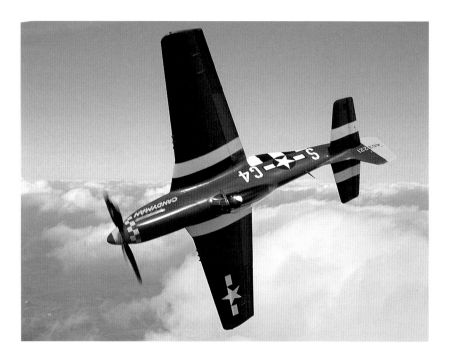

'I respected the P-51D but cannot say I loved it. Remember, I am talking about a fully armed combat aircraft in fighting trim. I made few flights when I did not take-off with a full load of fuel and ammunition. We always took off on the main fuselage tank (right behind the cockpit) and tried to retain the remainder of that tank to come home and land on. So we always, or almost always, had a half tank of fuel to slosh around unpleasantly during combat. A pilot who had not developed techniques to allow for this could get in serious difficulties during violent manoeuvres such as occurred during low-level bombing and strafing attacks. One of the endearing qualities of the old Curtiss P-40 was its unfailing habit of shaking the stick at the edge of a stall. The Mustang usually let you know that it had run out of flying speed by doing a violent snap roll – I never learned to appreciate that characteristic!'

Capt Jess Thompson, 55th FG, Wormingford, 1944

▲ ▶ P-51D Mustang

◀ P-51C Mustang

'I watched the Me 109s as we flew along and presently one detached himself to attack my section. I called a break to port into his attack and the flight did a beautiful job of breaking and staying together. The Hun kept up his attack and turned steeply to come in on my number four man's tail, so I pushed everything forward and dropped flaps to turn inside him. Through the early stages of the turn he out-turned me, but I pulled up and cork-screwed inside him and laid off a deflection shot which hit him hard enough to cause him to flick out of his turn. He started to split-ess, but my shots forced him to turn back the other way. Immediately I managed to get a few scattered strikes and he began to skid and slow up and prepare to bale out. I was closing in very rapidly so I dropped full flaps and throttled back completely. I was still overshooting him though, so I skidded and raked him without using my sights, for I could not hold my head behind the sight with such violent skids, and since I was so close, probably I could not have hit him with sights. Finally, I had to breakaway over him, and just then he baled out. I wish I could have hit the pilot for he was extremely good, and his loss would have meant a lot for our cause.'
Lt Willard Millikan, 4th FG, Debden, 1944

▲ P-51D of the 4th FG at Debden in 1945

◄ P-51D Mustang ▶

'We had eight ships up and spotted ten-plus Me 109s heading east on the deck. I lined up behind one that seemed to be a leader. As we came into range, my mind was suddenly filled with everything I had ever learned and practised for such a situation. Wait until his wings fill the ring sight. You're a little above him – pull the tit a bit out in front of his nose. Check the needle and ball – you don't want to be skidding. I squeezed the trigger and immediately everything from the four "fifties" converged on his engine, and he rolled over and went in. His wingman must have been surprised. I gave him a short burst. I guess the tracers passing over his wings was too much. He immediately jettisoned the canopy and baled out. I circled as he floated down, and when he landed, he calmly pulled in his chute, tucked it under his arm, waved and walked away!'
Lt Elmer O'Dell, 363rd FG, Azeville, 1944

▲ P-51D Mustang ▶

'El's Belle/Ginny was a P-51B-10 and I flew all of my missions with her. In June of 1944 I was offered a P-51D, but I preferred to keep the B-10. I checked out the D and flew a number of mock combat missions in it, but to me it didn't have the delicate response of the B-10, which had four 0.50-calibre guns. When they built the D they added another gun to each wing. To do so, they had to alter the configuration of the wing. I maintain this caused a small reduction in manoeuvrability. I guess it was a personal thing, for obviously most pilots thought otherwise.'
Lt Elmer O'Dell, 363rd FG, Azeville, 1944

◄ P-51D Mustang ▲

'As the Messerschmitts dove behind the other side of the huge bomber formation, I chose the least crowded area and flashed through the stream of B-17s and B-24s. I lost my flightmates, who had more sense than I did, and who pulled up and away from the stream as I penetrated it. Emerging from the cluster of bombers, who evidently recognised me as one of their own, I found two Bf 109s below me running to the southeast. They saw me as I bounced them, and pulled into a tight right turn. Following them, I fired a wide arching burst of tracer which ended in a fiery rain just in front of the leader. To my complete astonishment the pilot, seeing the hail of tracer fire immediately in front of him, jettisoned his canopy and bailed out!'

Capt Richard E Turner, 354th FG, Boxted, 1944

▲ P-51D Mustang and Bf 109G-10 ▶

'By far the best air-to-air fighter in the USAAF below 25,000 ft, the P-51D had a very good radius of action for the type of work we did in Europe. The acceleration from slow cruise to maximum performance was excellent compared with that of the competition. Its rate of roll was good and it manoeuvred easily to a learned hand. Dive and acceleration were rapid. Visibility in all directions was ample. As an instrument flying aircraft it was a bit touchy, and it could easily be over-controlled in turbulence. On the question of armament, it carried sufficient machine-guns. Why I say this is that after viewing numerous combat films where pilots fired at extreme range or over-deflected, I came firmly to a conclusion that one should fight for a combat position of ten degrees or less deflection. At close range – 250 yards or less – there is no doubt what would happen when the trigger was depressed: it was a matter of ducking the flying pieces after that.'
Col 'Hub' Zemke, 479th FG, Wattisham, 1944

◀ 364th FG pilots at Honington in 1945

▶ P-51D Mustang

'Our American allies had always claimed that the P-51 was a "hot ship" when compared to the Spitfire, primarily because it came in "over the hedge" at 120 rather than 90, but that caused us novice Mustang pilots no dramas at all. That said, there is no doubting that the P-51 was a great aircraft to fly, boasting a superb laminar-flow wing, huge range and generously proportioned cockpit. We ex-Spitfire pilots appreciated the latter enormously because after three-and-a-half hours in a Spitfire cockpit on a long-range bomber escort sortie, for example, one's lower half was well and truly "seized up".'

Flt Lt Raymond Baxter

▲ P-51A Mustang

▶ P-51D Mustang

'The P-51 was a most remarkable plane, but it wasn't as much fun to fly as the Spit. The Mustang was not quite as tight in the turn, but it was faster than the Spitfire or the 190 or the 109, and of course it had this remarkable range, but it could also turn pretty well. I've out-turned a Fw 190 in a Mustang, but more importantly the P-51 had superior performance from 30,000 ft down to the deck, and could do this 750 miles from home. When Göring saw Mustangs escorting the bombers to Berlin, he knew the war was over.'
Maj Jim Goodson, 4th FG, Debden, 1944

◀ P-51D Mustang ▲

▶ P-51C Mustang

'There were no tactical geniuses around to spread the gospel on how to stay alive in a dogfight with the Luftwaffe when we arrived in England in December 1943. Our training in the States had never envisaged seven-hour missions at 30,000 ft in weather where unfamiliarity with instruments would kill you faster than the enemy could.'
Lt Leonard 'Kit' Carson, 357th FG, Raydon, 1943

▲ P-51D Mustang ▶

de Havilland
MOSQUITO

'By the end of the war the Mosquito was if not the most famous aircraft of the RAF – the Spitfire was probably that – the most popular with the men who flew aeroplanes.' **Grp Capt Max Aitken, Banff Wing, 1945**

Truly an example of engineering ingenuity born out of the desperation of war, the legendary 'all-wooden' Mosquito was perhaps the best twin-engined fighter-bomber of its size to see action in World War 2. Built to replace the ageing Blenheim, the de Havilland design shared a similar birth with the Bristol bomber in that it was the result of a private venture by the former company, rather than in response to an Air Ministry requirement. A number of design facets adopted by the small team of de Havilland engineers at Salisbury Hall, in Hertfordshire, flew very much in the face of convention at the time, with the employment of a wooden fuselage and wings and the lack of any armament being perhaps the most radical. The design was initially presented to the Air Ministry in the autumn of 1938, but was politely rejected on the grounds of its unorthodox construction.

However, with the outbreak of war it soon became obvious that a shortage of light alloys from abroad could see aircraft production grind to a halt, thus making an all-wooden design very attractive. Approval was given to allow de Havilland to progress to a detailed design phase, and work began in December 1939. Three months later an order for 50 aircraft against Air Ministry Specification B.1/40 was received, and the first Mosquito took to the skies on 25 November 1940.

The sleek Merlin-powered design soon proved its worth during flight trials, possessing the manoeuvrability of a fighter and the payload of a medium bomber. The third of three prototypes built was completed as a photo-reconnaissance machine, the Mosquito's inherent high speed and high altitude attributes making it a natural for such demanding tasks. Indeed, this machine was the first Mosquito to see operational service when it performed a daylight sortie over southern France on 20 September 1941. The de Havilland design criterion of high speed through no armament was borne out on this mission when the PR Mk I easily outran three Bf 109Fs that attempted to intercept it.

The next version to enter service was the bomber optimised B Mk IV, the first examples of which were issued to No 2 Group's No 105 Sqn at Swanton Morley, in Norfolk, in November 1941. Considerably faster than the unit's previous Mk IV Blenheims, powered by inline rather than radial engines and made of wood instead of metal alloy, the Mosquito initially proved a challenging mount for both air- and groundcrew alike. New techniques had to be adopted for servicing on the ground, and new tactics evolved to ensure mission effectiveness in the air.

Work-ups on the new type were finally completed by the spring of 1942, and No 105 Sqn dropped its first bombs in anger on 31 May when four aircraft attacked Cologne during the aftermath of a '1000-bomber' raid on this target. Whilst the Mosquito was being successfully blooded as a bomber, the nightfighter version of the de Havilland design was also making its mark, having been developed from the second prototype of 1941. No 157 Sqn debuted the radar-equipped NF Mk II in April 1942, and the type went on to enjoy great success as a nocturnal raider protecting Bomber Command's vast fleet of 'heavies' as they journeyed deep into occupied Europe.

▲ Mosquito B IVs of No 105 Sqn banks away from the camera to reveal its snug-fitting bomb-bay doors

▶ Mosquitos at dispersal

'My section went right in for the corner of the east walls, while the others drew off a few miles and made their run-in on the north wall. Navigation was perfect and I've never done a better flight. It was like a Hendon demonstration. We flew as low and as slowly as possible, aiming to drop our bombs right at the foot of the wall. Even so, our bombs went across the first wall and across the courtyard, exploding on the wall at the other side. I dropped my own bombs from a height of ten feet, pulling hard on the stick. The air was thick with smoke, but of all the bombs dropped by both my section and the other, only one went astray.'
Wg Cdr I S 'Black' Smith, 140 Wing, Hunsdon, 1944

▲ Mosquito BIVs of No 105 Sqn, based at RAF Horsham St Faith, in 1942

▶ Mosquito T III

'For those of us who flew the Mosquitos on these attacks the memory of their versatility and their achievements will always remain. It would be impossible to forget such experiences as the thunderous din of 20 aircraft sweeping across the hangars as low as possible, setting course like bullets in tight formation for the enemy coast. The whole station would be out watching, and each leader would vie for the honour of bringing his formation lower across the aerodrome than anyone else. Nor would it be possible to forget the sensation of looking back over enemy territory and seeing your formation behind you, their racing shadows moving only a few feet below them across the earth's surface.'

Wg Cdr John Wooldridge, Marham Wing, 1944

◀ Mosquito T III ▲

'The first thing that struck one about the Mosquito was the beauty of line of the fuselage, tailplane, fin and engine cowlings. They all went together and made a lovely aeroplane. The cockpit cover also had a sweet line and the simplicity of the undercarriage and the treaded tyres set the whole thing off. The aircraft sat on the ground looking pert and eager and it was easy to become fond of – which was by no means true of all aeroplanes.'
Flg Off Frank Ruskell, No 109 Sqn, Wyton, 1943

▲ Mosquito T III ▶

'Several Fw 190s were seen flying above the aerodrome. We selected one which had its undercarriage down and attacked from its starboard beam. We opened fire with a two-second burst of cannon and machine-gun from 150 yards. The Fw 190 burst into flames and spiralled into the ground just off the eastern perimeter. Another Fw 190 with its wheels down was seen, and approached, but he must have seen us for he raised his undercarriage and climbed almost vertically. Attempting to follow him in the climb, we stalled. The enemy did a stall turn and dived to the deck, where we resumed the chase using maximum power to slowly close the range. The '190's sole evasive action consisted of flying as low and as fast as possible together with a bit of porpoising. We opened fire with several bursts at extreme range, and a few strikes were observed before my cannon ammunition was exhausted.'

Sqn Ldr J Gray, No 418 Sqn, Hunsdon, 1944

Boeing

B-17 FLYING FORTRESS

'After 25 missions, you cannot be without some sentiment for an aircraft that has been strapped to your back-side, sometimes for 10 hours at a stretch.' **Lt James Johnson, 100th BG, Thorpe Abbots, 1945**

No combat aircraft better sums up the might of the American aerial offensive in Europe than the Flying Fortress. It was the first US bomber to take the fight to Germany's heartland in countless daylight bombing raids on targets across the Third Reich, during which it tackled the might of the Luftwaffe head on. Those B-17Es and Fs that set off from bases in East Anglia in 1942 bound for occupied Europe were the end product of a controversial tactical philosophy championed by maverick USAAC Brig Gen 'Billy' Mitchell two decades earlier. He claimed that strategic bombing from high altitude was the way forward, and although his theories were mocked by senior officers at the time in both the Army and the Navy, the failure of his campaign to win over the military hierarchy of the day was due principally to the lack of a suitably advanced bomber, rather than any flaw in his ideas.

As the years passed by, however, manufacturers began to increase the size of their

aircraft thanks principally to the advent of stressed-metal construction and the greater power output offered by new radial and inline engines. One of those companies was Boeing of Seattle, who had furnished the Army with considerable numbers of small single-seat biplane fighters in the 1920s and 30s, but who realised that the big money was to be made in supplying large bombers. They had lost out with the YB-9 earlier in the decade, the order (for 48 aircraft) going to the Martin B-10, but this did not deter Boeing, who decided to make one last effort at cracking the multi-engine bomber nut through the privately produced Model 299. The Army, meanwhile, had already issued a request for a new bomber to replace the B-10, and Boeing seized its chance. On 28 July 1935 the first prototype took to the skies, and it was immediately dubbed the 'Flying Fortress' by the attending press.

The USAAC was impressed by the new bomber, and ordered an initial batch of 13 YB-17s, followed by the signing of a second contract for 39 near-identical B-17Bs. By mid-1940 the Flying Fortress had been further improved with the addition of two extra 0.50-in guns and the replacement of its GR-1820-51 engines of 1000 hp with R-1820-65 Cyclones of 1200 hp. Designated the B-17C, 20 of these aircraft were exported to Britain for service with the RAF as Fortress Mk Is.

Lessons learned from the European conflict saw Boeing beef up the armour fitted to future models of B-17, plus fit extra guns and self-sealing fuel tanks. The result of these changes was the B-17E, 512 of which were built in 1941/42, followed by the B-17F, which had a redesigned nose to incorporate a 0.50-in gun, plus a strengthened undercarriage to cope with increased bomb loads – the definitive Wright R-1820-97 engine also made its service debut with this variant. E- and F-models of the 97th Bombardment Group commenced the Eighth Air Force's daylight bombing campaign on 17 August 1942 when a mixed force struck targets in Rouen. Within 12 months huge formations 750 to 1000 bombers-strong were hitting targets on a near-daily basis, the B-17G, with its distinctive chin turret, becoming the mainstay of the Eighth's war of attrition right up to VE-Day – some 8680 of this model alone were built.

◀ An anonymous B-17F is captured in near-planform over its target in early 1944

▶ Waist gunners in an Eighth Air Force B-17G pose for the camera in mid-1944

'In my opinion the B-17 was the finest combat airplane the Air Force has ever had. It had one major disadvantage of course, in that it carried quite a small bomb load. Our normal loading was eight 500-lb bombs while operating from Australia; although there were bigger bombs in the theatre they were rarely used by my group. The B-17 was capable of carrying much more weight than we ever put into it: the problem was the configuration of the bay.'
Lt John Minahan, 28th BS/19th BG, Mareeba, 1942

▲ B-17G Flying Fortress ▶

▲ B-17Gs leave vapour trails as they head for Berlin in mid-1944

◀ B-17G Flying Fortress

'The reputation of the B-17 as a rugged fighting machine was well-known in the Air Force, and I was reassured of this on many occasions by what I saw and heard. Once, when our group had been attacked by fighters, an Me 109 collided with a B-17, taking off most of the rudder and left stabiliser, as well as slashing several holes in the fuselage. It was almost unbelievable that the B-17 could keep flying, but it did, and managed to make a safe landing back at base.'
Lt James Johnson, 100th BG, Thorpe Abbots, 1945

◀ B-17G Flying Fortress ▶

'When flying light and below oxygen altitudes I preferred flying the B-24. The cockpit was more comfortable and had a better layout and was much quieter than a B-17's. You had a better view of the ground too. But for combat give me the Fortress. It was much easier to fly in formation at high altitude. As far as I am aware the rest of the crew also felt the B-17 was better in combat. The bombardier and navigator definitely had much better visibility out of the nose. The interior of the B-17 seemed cleaner. Perhaps it was because it had mostly electric systems whereas the B-24 had hydraulics which were always a plumber's nightmare.'
Lt James Mynatt, 490th BG, Eye, 1944

▲ B-17G of the 390th BG at Framlingham in February 1944

▶ B-17G Flying Fortress and P-51D Mustang

▲ B-17E at Boeing in early 1942

▶ B-17G Flying Fortress

Mitsubishi
A6M ZERO

'The fighter seemed to stagger in the air, then fell off and dove into the ground. That was my third kill – the first American plane to be shot down in the Philippines.' ***Petty Officer First Class Saburo Sakai, Tainan Kokutai, Formosa, 1941***

Aside from the initial surprise of the early-morning raid on Pearl Harbor on 7 December 1941, perhaps the biggest shock for American forces in the Pacific was the outstanding performance of the Imperial Japanese Navy's main carrier fighter, the beautifully proportioned Mitsubishi A6M2 Type O Rei-sen, or Zero, as the world's press soon dubbed it. It was both fast and manoeuvrable, armed with two 20 mm cannon and two 7.7 mm machine guns, and possessed the incredible range of 1930 miles using a centreline drop tank – by comparison, the RAF's contemporary Spitfire I/II could manage barely 500 miles, the USAAF's P-40E 850 miles, also with the aid of a drop tank, and the F4F-3 Wildcat 830 miles.

Totally dismissed by British and American intelligence in the months leading up to the Pearl Harbor attack – despite written warnings from General Claire Chennault and his American Volunteer Group pilots in China, who had encountered early production A6M2 Model 11s assigned to land-based *Kokutai* – the Zero traced its origins back to an Imperial Navy Staff requirement issued in 1937 for an aircraft to replace the Mitsubishi A5M, then the main fleet fighter. Jiro Horikoshi had headed the team that was responsible for the earlier machine, and naturally he got to work draughting a design for the new 12-Shi replacement. Work progressed smoothly, and the first prototype flew on 1 April 1939.

The favoured engine at this stage in the aircraft's development was the Mitsubishi Zuisei 13, but due to its poor power rating of just 875 hp, the airframe had to be kept as light as possible – to the detriment of pilot safety, as no armour plating or self-sealing tanks were fitted to the fighter. By January 1940 it was realised that rival Nakajima's Sakae 12 engine was producing more horsepower, and more importantly was capable of further development. From that point on, various derivatives of the basic Sakae radial engine were to power all 10,500 Zeros built by Mitsubishi.

No fewer than eight different sub-types of Zero entered service, and the Sakae 12 of 950 hp eventually evolved into the water-methanol-injected 31-ko, which boasted 1200 hp. This figure paled when compared with the 2000 hp inline and radial engines employed by American fighters from late 1943 onwards, but the Zero remained a feared and worthy opponent due to its light weight – its main rival, the Hellcat, was twice as heavy!

The staple fighter of the Imperial Japanese Navy ace throughout World War 2, the Zero became progressively obsolescent as the Allied drive through the Pacific got into top gear. Indeed, by late 1944 most fighter squadrons were being forced to fly from land bases as the once proud carrier force had been all but sunk. Finally, in a last-ditch act, many Zeros were quickly converted into 'aerial bombs' and flung at the vast invasion fleets in *kamikaze* attacks off the Philippines, Iwo Jima and Okinawa.

▲ A6M5 Model 52 captured in the Pacific in late 1944

▶ A6M3 Model 32 captured at Buna, in New Guinea, in 1943

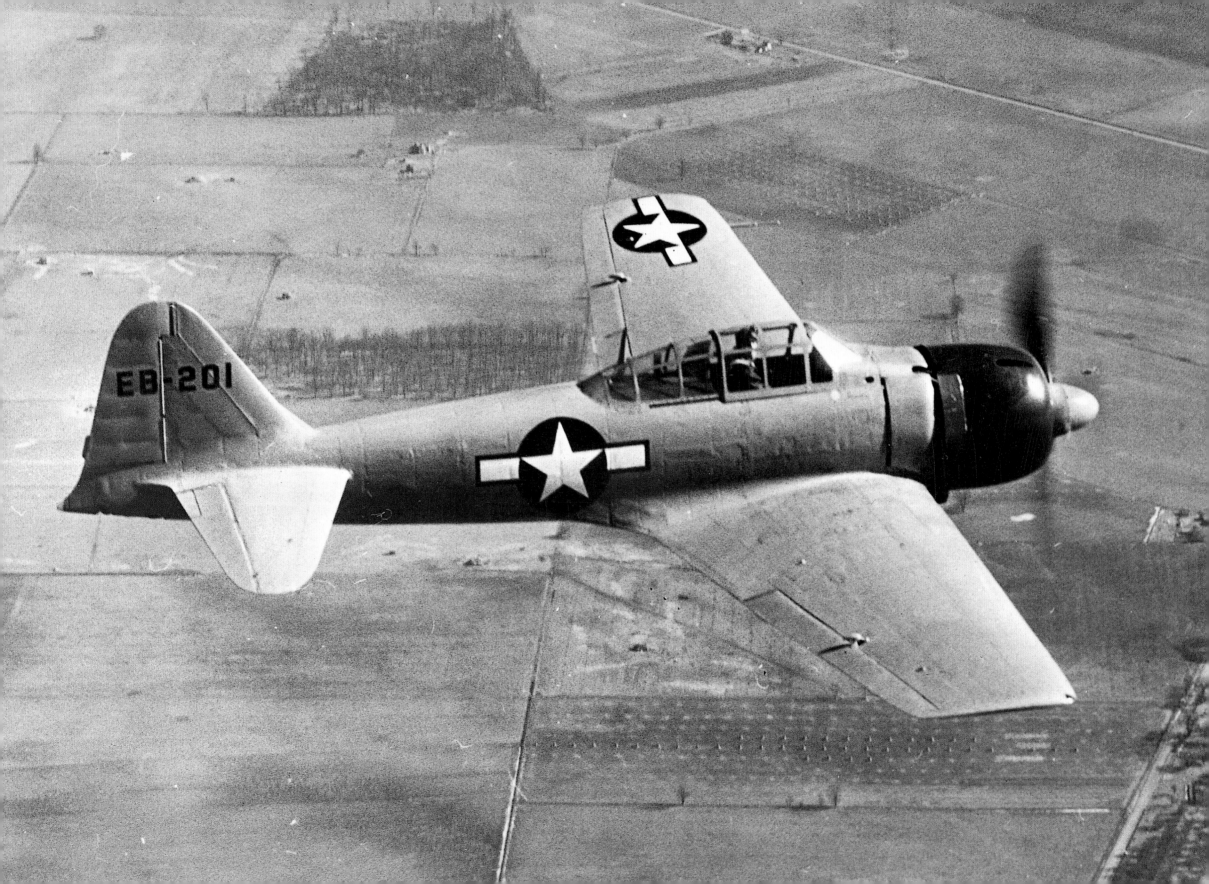

'The Zero excited me as nothing else had ever done before. Even on the ground it had the cleanest lines I had ever seen in an aeroplane. We now had enclosed cockpits, a powerful engine and retractable landing gear. Instead of only two light machine guns, we were armed with two machine guns and two heavy 20 mm cannon as well. The Zero had almost twice the speed and range of the A5M Claude, and it was a dream to fly. The aeroplane was the most sensitive I had ever flown, and even slight finger pressure brought instant response. We could hardly wait to meet enemy planes in this remarkable new aircraft.'

Petty Officer First Class Saburo Sakai, 12th Kokutai, central China, 1940

'The next day I returned to my first love – the Zero. I can never describe the wonder of the feelings which came back to me as I took the lithe fighter into the air. She handled like a dream. Just a flick of the wrist and she was gone! I went through all sorts of aerobatics, standing the Zero on her tail, diving, sliding off the wings. I was drunk with the air again.'
Ensign Saburo Sakai, Tainan Kokutai, Toyohashi, 1943

▲ A6M5 Model 52 ▶

'The Zero fighter, because of its low wing loading, has superior manoeuvrability to all our present service type aircraft. It is necessary to maintain a speed of over 300 mph (260 knots) indicated to successfully combat this airplane. Never attempt to dogfight the Zero. Never manoeuvre with the Zero at speeds below 300 mph indicated unless directly behind it. Never follow a Zero into a climb at slow speeds. Service types will stall out at the steep angle where the Zero has reached its most manoeuvrable speed. At this point it is possible for the Zero to complete a loop, putting it in a position for a rear-quarter attack.'

US Informational Intelligence Summary No 85, December 1942

▲ A6M3 Model 32s in the Pacific in 1943

◀ A6M5 Model 52 ▶

'I slammed my right foot against the rudder bar, skidding the Zero to the left. Then the stick, hard over to the left, rolling sharply. Sparkling lights flashed beneath my right wing, followed by a plummeting Hellcat. I cannot remember how many times the fighters attacked, nor how many times I rolled away. The perspiration rolled down my body, soaking my underclothes. My forehead was all beads of sweat, and it began to drip down onto my face. I cursed when the salty liquid trickled into my left eye. I couldn't take time to rub it with my hand. All I could do was to blink, try to keep the salt away, try to see. I was tiring much too quickly. I didn't know how I could get away. But it was very clear that these pilots weren't as good as their planes. An inner voice seemed to whisper to me. It repeated over and over the same words . . . speed . . . keep up your speed . . . forget the engine . . . burn it out, keep up your speed . . . keep rolling . . . never stop rolling . . .'

Lt(jg) Saburo Sakai, Yokosuka Air Wing, Iwo Jima, 1944

Douglas
SBD DAUNTLESS

'The Dauntless emerged with an almost legendary reputation as the most successful shipboard dive-bomber of all time – albeit success that perhaps owed more to the crews that flew it in truly dauntless fashion than to the intrinsic qualities of the aeroplane itself.' **Lt Cdr Eric 'Winkle' Brown, RAE Farnborough, 1944**

Unquestionably the most successful dive-bomber ever to see frontline service with any air arm, the Douglas SBD Dauntless was the scourge of the Japanese Imperial Fleet in the crucial years of the Pacific war. Almost single-handedly, 54 SBDs from the carriers *Enterprise* and *Yorktown* destroyed the heart of Adm Yamamoto's successful Pearl Harbor task force at the pivotal Battle of Midway on 4 June 1942, sending four large carriers to a watery grave. in the course of just 24 hours – this was a defeat from which the Japanese Navy never fully recovered.

The SBD of 1942 could trace its origins back to rival designs penned by the gifted pair of John Northrop and Ed Heinemann in the late 1930s. Improving on the basic principals employed in the design and construction of the USAAC's A-17 of 1936, Northrop produced the BT-1 for the US Navy in the spring of 1938. This revolutionary all-metal stressed-skin design exhibited airframe strength that made it an ideal candidate for adoption as a dive-bomber, replacing the antiquated biplane Curtiss SBC Helldiver in fleet and Marine Corps service. By the time the BT-1 had evolved into the BT-2 (the latter boasted a more powerful 1000 hp Wright Cyclone engine and inward-retracting mainwheels, amongst myriad detail changes and improvements), Northrop had been acquired by Douglas and the type was duly redesignated the SBD-1. The 'new' Douglas scout/dive-bomber differed from its Northrop progenitor in respect to its more streamlined fuselage shape and improved canopy, but it retained the design's trademark features – the broad wing with its horizontal centre section and sharply tapered outer panels with dihedral, and exaggerated perforated split flaps that doubled as dive brakes during steep bombing attacks.

Flight testing of the SBD-1 soon bore out the 'rightness' of the design, and with the delivery of the first of 57 production machines to VMB-2 in late 1940, the Marine Corps became the operators of the world's most advanced dive-bomber up to that point in history. By the spring of the following year the more definitive SBD-3 was in the process of being issued to frontline units, this version boasting self-sealing tanks, increased fuel capacity, a bullet-proof windscreen, armour protection, an uprated Wright R-1820-52 engine of

1000 hp and improved armament of two 0.50-in and two 0.30-in machine-guns. A total of 584 SBD-3s were built by Douglas at their El Segundo plant in California, and it was these machines that became the key combat aircraft in the Pacific in 1942/43. Indeed, in the crucial first six months of 1942, no American warplane saw more action than the Dauntless.

The SBD-4 differed only in detail changes from the -3, but the -5, produced in the new Douglas factory at Tulsa, Oklahoma, made use of the 1200 hp R-1820-60 engine and had increased ammunition capacity. This version proved to be the most populous Dauntless of them all, with 2409 being built. The USAAF also operated a significant number of SBD-3 and -4s, which they redesignated the A-24 – however, the success achieved by these land-based machines was minimal.

▲ Bombed up, a SBD-3 launches on its next mission in the Pacific in mid-1942

▶ Factory-fresh SBD-2s and -3s sit at Los Angeles municipal airport awaiting delivery to units in March 1941

'The first enemy fighter attacks were directed at the squadron leader in an attempt to put him out of action. After two passes, one of the enemy put several shots through the plane of Maj Henderson, and his SBD started to burn. From the actions of the leader it was apparent that he was hit and out of action. I was leader of the second box immediately behind the Major. As soon as it was apparent that the Major was out of action I took over the lead and continued the attack. Fighter attacks were heavy so I led the squadron down through a protecting layer of cloud and gave the signal to attack. On emerging from the cloud-bank the enemy carrier was directly below the squadron, and all planes made their runs. The diving interval was five seconds.'

Capt Elmer Glidden, VMSB-241, Midway Island, 1942

'In the vertical phase, from 12,000 ft down to bomb release, I was concentrating on adjusting the aircraft's heading to keep the cross hairs of my telescopic bomb sight on a red ball painted on the forward part of the flightdeck on the target ship. I concentrated on two things at this juncture; one was to watch the altimeter for 1500 ft coming up, the other was to push the electric bomb release button, and, at the same time, pull the manual bomb release lanyard at 1500 ft altitude. I did this to make doubly sure my bomb was released! Next, I concentrated on pulling out from my dive so that I would be just skimming the water when I regained the horizontal flight. Several seconds had passed after I had regained horizontal flight when my gunner shouted joyously over the intercom that my bomb had struck the target and that I should look back to see. I did so with satisfaction – but just for a moment, for then I concerned myself with evading ship's gunfire that manifested itself by shell splashes in the water in my vicinity.'

Lt Paul 'Lefty' Holmberg, VB-3, USS Yorktown, 1942

◀ SBD-5 Dauntless

▶ SBD-5 Dauntless and A6M5 Zero

◀ SBD-3 Dauntless off Guadalcanal in 1942

▶ SBD-5 Dauntless

'The Dauntless had established an enviable record for reliability and toughness, and its career in the Pacific had certainly been illustrious. Yet, from the performance standpoint it had been a very mediocre aeroplane, and having operated for much of the time in a non air superiority environment, one is left with a deep respect for its crews. I personally did not find the hidden quality in the Dauntless that I had sought on the strength of its remarkable operational reputation. I could only conclude that it was to be numbered among that handful of aeroplanes that have achieved outstanding success against all odds.'
Lt Cdr Eric 'Winkle' Brown, RAE Farnborough, 1944

Republic

P-47 THUNDERBOLT

'Back at Debden, I caught up with Blakeslee at debriefing. "I told you the Jug could out-dive them!" Grudgingly he conceded, "Well it damn well ought to be able to dive – it sure as hell can't climb!"' **Lt Jim Goodson, 4th FG, Debden, 1943**

The US aviation industry produced three great fighter designs to equip its burgeoning army air force during World War 2, and of this trio, Republic's P-47 Thunderbolt was easily the heaviest. That the 'Jug', as it soon became nicknamed, proved to be such a weighty aircraft is rather ironic for the original P-47, designed by Alexander Kartveli, was built to meet a 1940 USAAC requirement for a lightweight interceptor similar in size and stature to the Spitfire and Bf 109. To be powered by Allison's ubiquitous V-1710-39 1150 hp inline engine, the XP-47A was to boast just two 0.50-in machine guns as armament and lacked any protective armour or self-sealing tanks. However, the first combat reports filtering in from the war-torn European skies in mid-1940 proved the folly of a lightweight fighter design, and the USAAC modified its design requirements to include an eight-gun fitment, heavy armour plating and a self-sealing fuel system. Republic responded with an all-new design powered, crucially, by a turbocharged Pratt & Whitney R-2800 Double Wasp radial engine that produced 2000 hp – the question of the proposed fighter's all up weight was quietly ignored by USAAC.

Designated the XP-47B, the prototype was built around the bulky R-2800 engine and its associated turbocharger, which had stringent air ducting requirements. It completed its first flight on 6 May 1941, and despite the fighter initially suffering reliability problems with its powerplant, production of the Republic design forged ahead – the initial contract covered the purchase of 773 aircraft. In June 1942 the 56th FG became the premier unit to be equipped with the new P-47B, and six months later the group joined the Eighth Air Force in Britain to undertake the much needed escort role for the latter's growing B-17 bomber force. Initial encounters with German fighters were not particularly encouraging for the Thunderbolt pilots, for their aircraft was easily outmanoeuvred at low to medium altitudes, and its engine performance was rather lacklustre – the Jug's short range was also criticised.

The arrival of the first P-47Cs in mid-1943 addressed the problem of the aircraft's short combat radius, as this model could be fitted with an external tank. Slowly, as combat tactics evolved in units like the 56th and 78 FGs, pilots learnt how best to fly the Thunderbolt in

order to effectively counter the more nimble Luftwaffe fighters, and USAAF aces of the calibre of 'Hub' Zemke and 'Gabby' Gabreski began accruing substantial scores. Built to absorb much damage, and rock steady as a gun platform, the Thunderbolt was soon able to more than hold its own over German skies. The arrival of the definitive P-47D in late 1943 was followed shortly after by the advent of the 'bubble top' Thunderbolt, which then became the favoured mount over the 'razorback' Jug, thanks to its superior rearward visibility.

The ultimate Thunderbolt was the P-47N, whose uprated turbocharged R-2800-61 engine was capable of producing 2800 hp in combat configuration at 32,500 ft – ideal for intercepting high flying Axis interceptors. The N-model also had a slightly reduced armament of six guns, fitted into a newly strengthened and increased-span wing, which for the first time boasted internal tanks. Some 1816 P-47Ns were built (out of a total of 15,677 Thunderbolts), the majority of which were put to use escorting B-29s on bombing raids over the Japanese home islands.

▲ P-47D of the 356th FG moves in close during a bomber raid in early 1944

▶ P-47s are sandwiched between lines of P-51Bs at a US service Command depot somewhere in East Anglia in April 1944

'I checked Capt Don Blakeslee out on the P-47. Of course he didn't like it. It was daunting to haul seven tons of plane around the sky after the finger-tip touch needed for the Spit. I tried to sell Blakeslee on the opportunities this plane could open for us. "For one thing", I said, "they'll never be able to dive away from us again". He must have been listening. On 15 August 1943, Blakeslee was leading us over Belgium when we spotted a couple of Fw 190s. We attacked – as usual they dived away, and we followed. Admittedly it took a while. We jumped them at a little over 20,000 ft and Blakeslee was at 500 ft before he finally blew his victim out of the sky and into a suburb of Ostend. It was the first victory for the P-47.'

Lt Jim Goodson, 4th FG, Debden, 1943

▲ P-47G Thunderbolt
▶ P-47D Thunderbolt

'Hits registered all over his underside and the Me 110 came apart. After it blew up I began to pull back up to altitude when something flashed past my nose. It was a red-nosed Fw 190. I turned with him several times trying for a better position, and I finally got a decent angle for a head-on attack. Both the German and I held our fire until the range was point blank. He missed and I didn't! The Fw passed by with his engine smoking. By the time I got turned around the Fw was in a steep spiral, smoking badly, and the pilot finally baled out.'
Lt Donovan Smith, 56th FG, Horsham St Faith, 1943

CREW
Hugh Showers
Ben Wolever
Mac McGann
Stan Ostroskie

LT. A. H. BOMBERGER II

·MISS CARRIAGE·

'The orders were quite clear at this time, as they were always the same – "Stay With The Bombers!" But sometimes you cannot obey orders. I was Blue 3 and we were on our way out escorting the bombers home. Two Me 109s came down out of the sun right in front of us with their bellies to us. A perfect angle for a kill I thought. I called them in but my leader told us to "Let them go!" I watched them continue down and start a roll-out to the left. That's when I saw that there were two Jugs right in front of them if they continued their flight path. I rolled out to the right and started down, knowing full well that I would be in trouble for breaking a direct order to leave them alone and for breaking escort. I shot one Messerschmitt down, but upon my return to Halesworth I was fined £5.00 for breaking formation.'
Lt Harold Comstock, 56th FG, Halesworth, 1943

▲ P-47D of the 56th FG at Boxted in 1944. Lt Bomberger's aircraft also shared its nickname with a 349th BS B-17F

◀ P-47D Thunderbolt

▲ P-47D Thunderbolt

▶ P-47G Thunderbolt

Messerschmitt
Bf 109G

'The pilot who sees the other first already has half the victory.'
Hauptmann Erich Hartmann, Gruppenkommandeur I./JG 52, Russian Front, 1944

Numerically the most abundant fighter produced by either side during World War 2, the Messerschmitt Bf 109 was to form the backbone of the Jagdwaffe on both the Eastern and Western Fronts, as well as in the Mediterranean and North Africa. Of the eight distinct sub-types within the huge Bf 109 family, the most populous was the G-model, of which over 30,000 were built between 1941 and 45. The Germans were always attempting to crank more performance out of the small fighter, and as an example of this no fewer than nine major sub-variants were produced of the G-model alone, ranging from the basic G-0 of late 1941, through to the G-14 of May 1945.

Turning the clock back ten years, the original Dipl-Ing Willy Messerschmitt-designed Bf

109 V1 flew for the first time on 28 May 1935, powered by a 695 hp Rolls-Royce Kestrel engine. By the time the initial production-standard fighters were issued to the Luftwaffe in the spring of 1937, the Bf 109 had been re-engined with the Junkers Jumo 210 inline powerplant. Another 18 months, and two sub-types, were to pass before the originally specified Daimler-Benz DB 601 engine was at last made available in sufficient quantities to allow Messerschmitt to commit the outstanding E-model to production in mid-1938. From that moment on, the Bf 109 and the DB 600 series engine would prove to be inseparable.

From the first hours of *Blitzkrieg* in Poland on 1 September 1939, the Bf 109 was charged with securing aerial supremacy for the marauding Wehrmacht as it overran virtually all of mainland Europe in a matter of months. Only when the Luftwaffe attempted to gain control of the skies over Britain was the E-model found wanting – this was as much due to the aircraft's limited range as to the tactics employed by both the RAF and the Luftwaffe. As good as it was, the Emil was being progressively bettered in virtually all aspects of aerial combat by the Spitfire as 1941 progressed, so Messerschmitt updated and improved the breed with the introduction of the F-model, which boasted a more aerodynamically refined nose section covering the DB 601E engine, rated at 1350 hp. Over an 18-month period over 2000 were built, before production switched to the most durable of all wartime Bf 109s, the Gustav.

Designed around the 1475 hp DB 605 engine, the G-model also introduced cockpit pressurisation – crucial from late 1942 onwards when the fighter *Gruppen* struggled to repel high-altitude USAAF daylight bomber raids. A variety of integral and podded machine guns and cannon of various calibre were also made available for use with the Gustav, as were unguided rockets and mortars. These modifications, along with engine updates, were often issued to frontline units in *Rüstsätze* (field conversion) kit form, resulting in virtually no two G-models ever being truly identical. Despite the advent of better fighters like the Fw 190/Ta 152 and the jet-powered Messerschmitt Me 262, the Bf 109G still remained an able fighter right up to VE-Day.

◄ Factory-fresh Bf 109G-1s in mid-1942

► Bf 109G-6/U2 formerly of 1./JG 1, captured at RAF Manston on 21 July 1944

▶ Bf 109G-10

▼ Bf 109G-1 shot down in Russia in late 1942

'I always flew the Messerschmitt 109, beginning with the G-6 and ending with the K-14. The Gustav was far more powerful than the Friedrich, but any advantage was more than offset by its heavier armament. The G-10, for example, had a 30 mm cannon with devastating efficiency. It was also the fastest of all the Gustavs, with an excellent rate of climb, and it handled well in all flight regimes. I always felt comfortable, and the master of any situation, in my trusty "Beule".

Hauptmann Erich Hartmann, Gruppenkommandeur I./JG 52, Russian Front, 1945

'I shall make a frontal attack. The Yank is focused in my sights. He grows rapidly larger. I reach for the firing buttons on the stick. Tracers come whizzing past my head. They have opened up on me! Fire! I press both buttons, but my aim is poor. I can see only a few hits register in the right wing. I almost scrape the fat belly as I dive past. Then I am caught in the slipstream, buffeted about so violently that for a moment I wonder if my tailplane has been shot away. I climb up steeply and break away to the left. Tracers pursue me, unpleasantly close. Damn all this metal in the air!'

Oberleutnant Heinz Knoke, Staffelkapitän 5./JG 52, Jever, 1943

◀ Bf 109G-10 ▲

'I open fire on a Liberator from a little below. It immediately starts burning and sheers off to the right as it falls away from the formation. I come in again to attack from above the tail, and then turn for another frontal attack, firing from ahead and below the steeply diving Liberator. My aim has never been better. Suddenly there is an explosion, and the blazing crate disintegrates into a shower of wreckage above my head. For a few minutes I am in danger of collision with falling engines or spinning, flaming wings. That would mean certain disaster for me. Acting quickly, I slam the stick hard over into the left corner and go into a power dive. The falling fuselage of the Liberator misses me by inches as it hurtles into the depths. This was number five kill.'
Oberleutnant Heinz Knoke, Staffelkapitän 5./JG 52, Jever, 1943

▲ Badly battered Bf 109G-10 captured in Germany in 1945

▶ Bf 109G-2

'I've fully integrated all the motions in air combat and with difficult manoeuvres. It begins as I close with the enemy. I've now come so far that I can keep control of the Bf 109 in any situation, even in the tightest turns and at the lowest possible speeds. In combat I make all my motions unconsciously. This lets me concentrate fully on the attack, and fly my plane as though I had wings.'

Hauptmann Hans-Joachim Marseille, Staffelkapitän 3./JG 27, Quotaifiya, 1942

▲ Bf 109G-2 ▶

'The Bf 109 always brought to my mind the adjective "sinister". It has been suggested that it evinced characteristics associated with the nation that conceived it, and to me it looked lethal from any angle, on the ground or in the air – once I had climbed into its claustrophobic cockpit it felt lethal!'

Lt Cdr Eric 'Winkle' Brown, RAE Farnborough, 1944

▲ Bf 109G-10

▶ A captured Bf 109G-2 is evaluated in 1944

'One of my rashest ventures was to fly the Bf 109G-12 tandem two-seater from the rear cockpit with no one in the forward cockpit. I was interested to ascertain what sort of view the instructor had for landing. The answer was none! I had to make three very frightening attempts before regaining terra firma. The periscopic sight in the rear cockpit was of no use whatsoever in the vital final stage of flare, touch-down and landing run. One can only assume that Luftwaffe instructors finding themselves in a Bf 109G-12 acquired a fatalistic acceptance of an inevitable reliance on their pupils for the finale of each training flight. I would certainly not recommend the ultimate solution that I adopted of a split-S turning dive at the runway and then a burst of power to avoid cratering the tarmac, and making tail-up contact on the mainwheels. After the tail dropped it was anybody's guess as to the direction in which the aircraft was heading. I certainly had not the vaguest idea.'

Lt Cdr Eric 'Winkle' Brown, RAE Farnborough, 1944

Grumman
F6F HELLCAT

'The Hellcat was without a doubt the best, and most popular, naval fighter of the period.'
Lt Cdr Stanley Orr, Officer Commanding No 804 Sqn, HMS Emperor, 1944

When one thinks of American aces of World War 2, one's mind is immediately filled with images of gaudily-painted P-51s prowling the skies over war-torn Germany. Surely the combination of beautiful flying characteristics and overwhelming strength in numbers must have meant that the superb North American Mustang was the premier US 'ace-maker' of World War 2? The plain and simple answer is no – that mantle rests with Grumman's rotund F6F Hellcat. The bold stats are as follows; of the 1300 US pilots to claim five or more victories in combat, 305 did so in a Hellcat and 275 in a Mustang.

The Hellcat was probably always destined to be a winner, as it embodied the early lessons learnt by users of Grumman's previous fleet

fighter, the F4F Wildcat, in the Pacific, as well as general pointers from the RAF's experience in Europe. The original design for the Hellcat actually dated back to late 1940, and the US Navy placed an advance order for the fighter in June 1941. Modifications to the 'paper' aircraft in light of combat reports, particularly from the Battle of the Coral Sea, saw Grumman lower the wing centre section to enable the undercarriage to be wider splayed, the fitment of more armour-plating around the cockpit to protect the pilot and an increase in the fighter's ammunition capacity for its six 0.50 in machine guns.

Less than a year after the Navy placed its order, the prototype XF6F-1 made its first flight. It was soon realised that a more powerful engine was needed to give the fighter a combat edge, so a Pratt & Whitney R-2800-10 was installed, resulting in the F-1 being

redesignated an F-3. The Wildcat's ability to stave off the enemy was being severely tested by this stage in the war, and the Hellcat was immediately rushed into production following the successful test flight of the re-engined prototype.

The first squadron to see action in the F6F-3 was VF-5 aboard USS *Yorktown* in August 1943, and from this point on, the question of aerial supremacy in the Pacific was never in doubt. The Hellcat was to serve aboard virtually all the US Navy's fleet carriers in varying numbers, and was credited with the destruction of 4947 aircraft up to VJ-Day. All the leading Navy aces of the war including Cdr David McCampbell (34 kills), Lt Eugene A Valencia (23 kills) and Lt Cecil E Harris (22 kills) flew Hellcats, with the premier fighter squadron in the Pacific, VF-15, downing 310 enemy aircraft with the rugged Grumman.

Amazingly, only three major variants of the F6F were produced – the -3, of which 4423 were built between October 1942 and April 1944, the improved -5 day fighter and the specialised -3N and -5N nightfighters.

The Royal Navy's Fleet Air Arm (FAA) was also a great believer in the Hellcat, procuring almost 1200 though lend-lease arrangements from 1943 through to 1945. Operating both main day fighter types as the Hellcat I (-3) and II (-5), 12 squadrons saw action with both the Home and Pacific Fleets. One of the first units to blood the FAA's Hellcats in combat was No 804 Sqn during attacks on the *Tirpitz* in April 1944.

▲ F6F-5s of VC-6 aboard USS *Tripoli* in 1945

▶ F6F-5 of VF-1 aboard USS *Bennington* in 1945

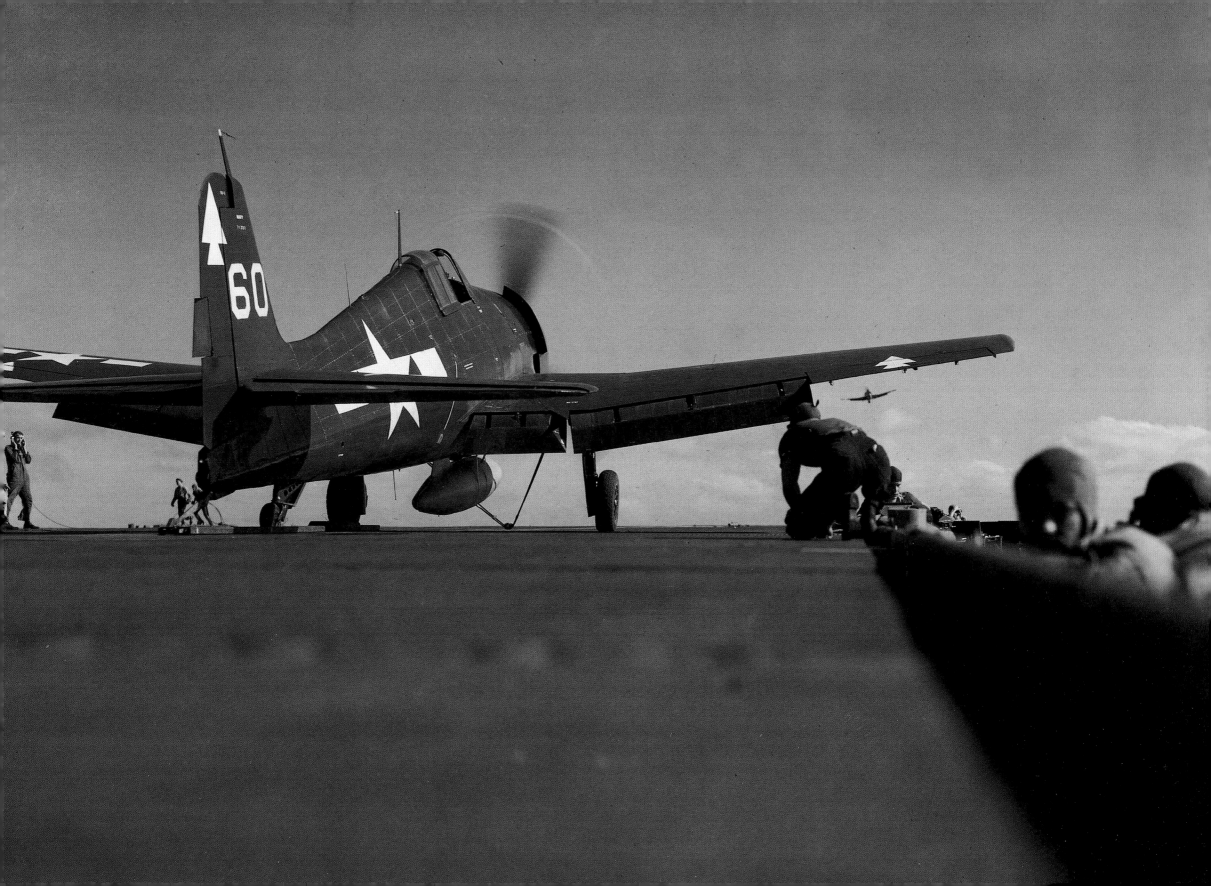

'The Hellcat suffered none of the Corsair's stall and visibility problems, being an easy aircraft both to fly and to deck land. It bestowed upon its pilot immense confidence, which was an important thing in those days as you usually had your hands more than full coping with the enemy!'
Lt Cdr Stanley Orr, Officer Commanding No 804 Sqn, HMS Emperor, 1944

▲ F6F-5 of Reserve Escort Carrier Group 71 after a heavy landing
aboard USS *Cabot* in February 1949

◀ F6F-3 Hellcat

▶ F6F-5 Hellcat

'After pulling up and over, I picked out another "Judy" on the edge of the formation. It was mildly manoeuvring, and the Japanese rear gunner was squirting away as I came down from behind. I worked in close, gave him a burst and set him afire quickly. The "Judy" headed for the water, trailing a long plume of smoke. I pulled up again to find two more "Judys" flying a loose wing. I came in from the rear to send one of them down burning. Dipping my Hellcat's wing, I slid over on the other and got it on the same pass. It caught fire also, and I could see the rear gunner continuing to pepper away at me as he disappeared in an increasingly sharp arc downward. For a split second I almost felt sorry for the little bastard.'

Lt(jg) Alex Vraciu, VF-16, USS Lexington, *1944*

▲ F6F-5 Hellcat

◀ F6F-5 Hellcat

'I snapped back in a tight turn. The manoeuvre startled the enemy pilots as I climbed at them from below, swinging into a spiral. I was surprised: they didn't scatter. The lead fighter responded with an equal spiral, matching my manoeuvre perfectly. Again I spiralled, drawing it closer this time. The opposing fighters refused to yield a foot. This was something new. An Airacobra or a P-40 would have been lost trying to match me in this fashion, and not even the Wildcat could hold a spiral too long against a Zero. But these new Hellcats – they were the most manoeuvrable enemy planes I had ever encountered.'
Lt(jg) Saburo Sakai, Yokosuka Air Wing, Iwo Jima, 1944

▲ F6F-3 of VF-16 launches from USS *Lexington* in late 1943

▶ F6F-3 Hellcat

◀ F6F-5 Hellcat and A6M Zero

'I don't know exactly how long the fight lasted. It was a long one – my guess is three to five minutes. I finished the fight with four Zekes on my tail arguing about who'd kill me. I used my last ditch manoeuvre: shove the stick forward as hard as I could with the throttle two-blocked and pitch full low. Nobody could follow that and shoot, so you gained at least a few seconds to think. As soon as I was headed straight down, I put the stick hard to the right for a spiral because the Zero couldn't turn well to the right at high speed. I lost them."

Ens Paul Drury, VF-27, USS Princeton, 1944

▲ F6F-3 Hellcat

◀ F6F-5 Hellcat

▶ USS *Yorktown's* hangar deck is full of VF-5 F6F-3s in this late 1943 photograph

▲ F6F-5s of VC-6 aboad USS *Tripoli* in 1945

▶ F6F-3

Vought
F4U CORSAIR

'After finding the F4U more responsive to persuasion than dominance, "Dog Ears" Coleman, an 'ole country boy serving with VF-12, had remarked, "This plane is as co-operative as a hog on ice". Thus the F4U was known for a long time as the Hog.' **Lt Cdr Tommy Blackburn, VF-17, Floyd Bennett Field, 1943**

Recognised as the best carrier fighter to see combat during World War 2, Vought's distinctive F4U Corsair was for a long time considered to be too dangerous to operate with the US fleet. It took the Fleet Air Arm's success with the type from its smaller 'flat tops' to convince senior officers in the US Navy of the fighter's 'blue water' ability, but once it was issued to frontline squadrons, naval aviators were credited with downing 2140 enemy aircraft for the loss of just 189 Corsairs – all in just 16 months of carrier operations from April 1944 to August 1945!

Designed as a lightweight fighter tailored around the most powerful piston engine then available, the prototype XF4U-1 was ordered by the US Navy in June 1938 following a study of Vought's V-166 proposal. In order to harness the immense power of the Pratt & Whitney XR-2800 Double Wasp engine proposed by Vought, the largest diameter propeller ever fitted to a fighter up to that point in aeronautical history had to be bolted on the front of the prototype. Sufficient ground clearance for the prop, whilst still maintaining a short, strong undercarriage leg system was achieved through the use of a distinctive inverted gull wing. Outputting 1850 hp at take-off, the Double Wasp engine bestowed upon the XF4U-1 outstanding performance figures when the type was first flown on 29 May 1940.

The future looked superb for the aircraft, but later that year it was decided to incorporate modifications resulting from the lessons learned in combat over Europe - these 'mod's' detrimentally affected the initial design. The primary cause for concern was the shifting of the cockpit aft by some three feet in order to allow fuel tanks, previously sited in the wings,

to be moved into the centre fuselage – this change was precipitated by the installation of two more 0.50-in guns in the wings. When the type finally began to enter fleet service as the F4U-1 Corsair in September 1942, the US Navy soon realised that the changes had rendered the aircraft unsuitable for deck operations due to the restrictive view on offer to the pilot when landing back aboard ship. Criticism was also levelled at the 'bouncy' landing gear fitted to the fighter, and whilst Vought were busy rectifying these crucial faults, virtually all the -1s delivered to the Navy were in turn passed on to the Marines.

Embroiled in a bitter 'island hopping' war in the Pacific, the 'Corps were operating from basic strips carved out of virgin jungle – unhospitable territory that the rugged Corsair took in its stride. VMF-124 debuted the F4U-1 over Guadalcanal in February 1943, and its pilots were soon enjoying a dominance over the previously near-unbeatable Zero – something that the Wildcat had failed to achieve. The Fleet Air Arm had also commenced operations with the Corsair in 1943, and within 12 months had seen combat from carrier decks with the type. Vought, meanwhile, had modified their design into the F4U-1A, which had a raised cockpit, covered by a bubble canopy, a less springy undercarriage and improved aerodynamic devices on the wings to increase stability upon landing. With these changes the Corsair was deemed suitable for deck operations with the US Navy.

The final version to see service during World War 2 was the awesome F4U-4, which had an uprated R-2800-18W or -42W engine, four-bladed propeller, improved cockpit layout and 20 mm cannon as an option in place of the standard battery of six 0.50-in machine-guns.

▲ Corsair IIs of a Fleet Air Arm training unit seen aboard an unidentified Home Fleet carrier in early 1944

▶ F4U-1Ds of VF-84 prepare to launch from USS *Bunker Hill* against targets in the Japanese Home Islands in February 1945

▲ FG-1D Corsair ▶

'The airplane was huge, far bigger than any fighter I had ever seen. Most of it seemed to be engine. As soon as possible, I fired up the big bird and began going through the pre-take-off checks the moment the 2000-hp engine was warm. At length, I gingerly taxied forward, cursing the extremely poor ground visibility of this and all Navy fighters of the day; with its long nose stretching an unprecedented 12 ft in front of my windshield, the F4U was the champ of champs in this regard. Sinuous forward movement was an absolute must if I wanted to see anything out ahead.'

Lt Cdr Tommy Blackburn, VF-17, Floyd Bennett Field, 1943

▲ 'Leathernecks' get full aerial support from their flying brethren during the hand-to-hand fighting on Okinawa in April 1945

▶ F4U-1A Corsair and P-40K Kittyhawk

'He dove down even lower to pick up speed, getting down to between 10 to 25 ft above the water. I was then at about 100 ft, with my wingman on my right wing. I was wide open for at least ten minutes and wasn't gaining on him. After we landed, my wingman told me that at the time sparks were coming out of my exhaust. The F4U's top speed was 405 mph at sea level, so the Zeke was also moving at about that speed. I was probably gaining a little on him, but I couldn't stay wide open much longer or I would burn up my engine. If I fixed my sights on him in level position my bullets would hit the water behind him. By raising my nose the bullets would go straight for about 800 to 900 ft, then drop downward due to gravity. Even if he was 800 ft away, I would have to raise my sights above him. My plan was to lob the bullets into him so I fired another short burst. He hit the water and bounced back up and kept going. I knew I had the right angle on raising my nose so I fired again. He hit the water again and bounced back up. Again I fired and he hit the water and came back up. The fourth time, however, he went down to stay.'
Lt Joe D Robbins, VBF-8, USS Shangri-La, 1945

▲ F4U-1D on final approach to its carrier in the Pacific in early 1945

◄ FG-1D Corsair

▶ F4U-1A Corsair

'With the Corsair you felt like you were literally strapped into an armchair in your sitting room, the cockpit was that large. You honestly felt like a "king" sitting up there, with virtually unlimited visibility through the bubble canopy of the Mark II. We flew those aircraft very hard, and just to illustrate this point, a little after the Sumatra show we ventured northward to Okinawa for Iceberg, where I came across an airfield full of the latest spec F4U-4s in glossy sea blue at Manus, in the Admiralty Islands, awaiting shipment back to the US. I found the US Navy Officer in charge of this operation and asked him what was occurring. He told me that they were being returned to the States for overhaul and repair, prior to being sent to the frontline again. I enquired as to their individual service use per airframe and he replied that they had seen about 500 hours of flying each. I was astonished, and replied that our Corsair IIs had accrued nearly 2000 each, and were no nearer an overhaul or deep service than the day they were built! I ventured a swap whereby I took one of his non-serviced machines in place of my old crate, and he replied, "Sure bud, you can have any one you like. Any guy going up to the 'sharp end' can take anything he wants!" Sadly, I fear my admiral would have spotted the F4U-4's glossy blue scheme sat amongst the ranks of sea grey Corsair IIs on Victorious!'

Maj Ronnie Hay, No 47 Wing, HMS Victorious, 1945

◀ F4U-1A Corsair ▲

▶ FG-1D Corsair

Lockheed
P-38 LIGHTNING

'With its inherent stability the P-38 was extremely easy to fly, and once trimmed for straight and level flight, it was a hands-off airplane – what complete comfort for a combat plane.' **Lt Royal Frey, 20th FG, Wittering, 1944**

The most distinctive looking Allied fighter to serve in the frontline during World War 2, the P-38 Lightning was Lockheed's first venture into the world of high performance military aircraft – it was perhaps this very lack of experience, and therefore preconceptions, in fighter design that allowed the Burbank, California, based company to arrive at its revolutionary twin boom layout. Keen to break into the lucrative military marketplace, Lockheed had eagerly responded to the USAAC's 1937 Request for Proposals for the acquisition of a long-range interceptor, designated X-608. The new machine had to have a top speed in excess of 360 mph at 20,000 ft, the ability to take-off and land over a 50-ft obstacle within 2200 ft, the reliability to fly at full throttle for over an hour non-stop, and boast an armament double that fitted into the Curtiss P-36A Hawk – the USSAC's frontline fighter of the period.

No aircraft then in service – or under development – with any air arm across the globe could come close to matching these performance figures. Lockheed's design team, led by H L Hibbard and Clarence 'Kelly' Johnson, considered that any new type proposed by their department would have to be twin-engined in order to allow the fighter to match the top speed or rate of climb stipulated by the specification. The powerplant chosen for the fighter was the much-vaunted (at the time) 960 hp Allison V-1710, as used in the contemporary P-40 and later P-51A.

As mentioned earlier, in order to accommodate the engines a novel twin boom, central nacelle and tricycle undercarriage layout was adopted in the XP-38, as well as butt-joined and flush riveted all-metal skins (and flying surfaces) – all a first for any US fighter

aircraft. The XP-38's test programme progressed well following its maiden flight on 27 January 1939, and aside from some adjustment made to the tailplane incidence, elevator mass balancing and wing root fairings in an effort to try and cure tail buffeting encountered during service trials with the YP-38, definitive frontline P-38s differed little from the prototype aircraft throughout the type's six-year production run. The tail buffeting problem was never truly overcome.

The appellation 'Lightning' was bestowed upon the P-38 by the RAF when the type was ordered in 1940 by the British Purchasing Commission, and adopted by the Americans with the advent of the E-model in mid-1941. Although no less than 667 were initially requested, the RAF was so disappointed in the performance of the three unsupercharged aircraft it received in late 1941 that the entire order was cancelled the following summer – the supercharger fitted to the V-1710 was still designated a classified item by the US government at this point in the war, and thus restricted from overseas sale.

However, the definitive P-38 models – namely the E, F, H and J – fitted with supercharged Allison engines, improved Fowler flaps and boasting extra fuel tank, proved more than a match for Axis fighters across the globe. Indeed, the Lightning was credited with more kills in the Pacific theatre than any other USAAF type, and the two top scoring American pilots of World War 2 achieved all their kills on P-38s – Maj Richard I Bong, who claimed 40 victories with the Fifth Air Force, and Maj Thomas B McGuire with 38 kills, (also scored with the Fifth in the Pacific).

▲ Newly arrived from America, a P-38J is 'steam cleaned' prior to reassembly in April 1944

▶ P-38L 'droop snoot'

California Cutie

'The value of the P-38 in the southwest Pacific can be illustrated by an incident related at the end of the war by a veteran of the 8th Fighter Group. One day in 1945 cries of distress were heard over the radio somewhere above the China Sea. "My engine's hit, I'm losing coolant - what'll I do?" Savvy P-38 pilots in the air at the time tried to advise the obviously green fellow in distress. "Calm down and feather it." Then came the dejected reply, "Feather, hell. I'm flying a P-51!"'
John Stanaway, P-38 historian

◀ P-38J Lightning ▲

'Oh, Hedy Lamarr is a beautiful gal
and Madeleine Carroll is too,
But you'll find if you query, a different theory
amongst any bomber crew
For the loveliest thing of which one could sing
(this side of the Pearly Gates)
Is no blonde or brunette of the Hollywood set
But an escort of P-38s.

'Yes, in the days that have passed, when the tables were massed
with glasses of scotch and champagne
It's quite true that the sight was a thing to delight
Us, intent upon feeling no pain.
But no longer the same, nowadays, in this game
When we head north from Messina Straits
Take the sparkling wine – every time just make mine
an escort of P-38's.

'Byron, Shelley and Keats run a dozen dead heats
Describing the view from the hills,
of the valleys in May when the winds gently sway
In the air it's a different story;
We sweat out our track through the fighter and flak
We're willing to split up the glory
Well, they wouldn't reject us, so Heaven protect us
and, until all this shooting abates,
Give us courage to fight 'em – one other small item -
An escort of P-38's.'
Anonymous radioman on a Fifteenth Air Force B-17, Italy, 1944

◀ P-38F of the 94th FS/1st FG at Youk las Bains, North Africa, in late 1942

▶ P-38J Lightning

'While in the pilots' lounge at Santa Maria Air Base, California, I overheard three P-38 student pilots scorning their airplane. They were saying the P-38 would not operate above 25,000 ft, or if it would, their instructor would not take them. I found out their instructor's name and cleared a flight with the students. My briefing was short and to the point: "We're going to take this four-ship formation up and we will continue to climb until one of you say 'Uncle'." With that we took off. At 42,800 ft indicating on the altimeter, I heard a garbled "uncle" being transmitted by a throat mike. One hundred per cent oxygen under pressure made it difficult to speak at high altitude. The formation was climbing at 500 ft per minute when the flight was terminated. That flight convinced them that the P-38 was a high altitude aircraft.'

Lt Frank Shearin Jr, formerly of the 343rd FG, the Aleutians, 1943

◀ P-38J Lightning ▲

'Admittedly, the P-38 was outperformed by the P-47 and P-51 in the skies over Europe, but many of its difficulties were the result of unnecessary design deficiencies and the slow pace of both the AAF and Lockheed in correcting them. One can only ponder about how much more rapidly the troubles would have been remedied if the slide-rule types had been flying the plane in combat against the Luftwaffe. But I will always remember the P-38 with the greatest fondness. Even with all her idiosyncrasies, she was a real dream to fly.'
Lt Royal Frey, 20th FG, Wittering, 1944

▲ P-38J Lightning ▶

'Lt Brown took violent evasive action, doing dives, zooms, skids, rolls and other various manoeuvres, but the German continued to follow about 50 yards behind, firing continually. In the meantime, I moved to a position about 400 yards behind the Me 109, and using full throttle was able to work up on his tail to a position about 150 yards behind him. I had already fired three or four high shots of one or two seconds' duration at the German, but with no noticeable results. Finally, Lt Brown tried a skidding barrel roll, but the Messerschmitt followed and put a long burst into Lt Brown's right engine, causing heavy, brown smoke to pour out. As the German fired, I fired a five-second burst at no deflection from the inverted position. His engine burst into flames and pieces of the plane flew all over the sky. I passed within 50 ft of him and observed fire from the engine streaming back over the fuselage. Lt Brown feathered his right engine and was able to make it back to our home base.'

Lt Joe Myers, 55th FG, Nuthampstead, 1943

▲ P-38J Lightning

▶ P-38J of the Eighth Air Force, England, 1944

Grumman

TBF/TBM AVENGER

'I did not fancy this Avenger when I first climbed in and started up. The engine clanked like a Tin Lizzy, the plane shook and the finishing of the airframe was, I thought poor. But first impressions turned out to be wrong. I soon began to like it, and by the time I was in carriers, I was thoroughly impressed with its all-round performance.' **Lt Donald Judd, No 832 Sqn, NAS Quonset Point, 1943**

Although Grumman of New York was principally responsible for producing the majority of the US Navy's fighter aircraft during World War 2, the company also designed and constructed the best carrier-based torpedo bomber of the conflict in the shape of the TBF/TBM Avenger. Built as a replacement for the Douglas TBD Devastator, two prototype XTBF-1s were ordered from Grumman in April 1940, along with the rival XTBU-1 design from Consolidated, which eventually evolved into the less than successful TBY Sea Wolf. Grumman guru Bill Schwendler, and his team, saw their rotund prototype take to the skies for the first time on 1 August 1941, the aircraft's portly appearance being due to its capacious internal bomb bay which was large enough to contain the biggest (22-in) torpedo in the Navy arsenal – it also boasted a crew of three, all of whom occupied generous stations beneath the impressive 'glasshouse' canopy.

Powered by the ever-reliable Wright R-2600 Cyclone radial engine, the Avenger was also well-armed, with the pilot operating a forward firing 0.30-in machine-gun that fired through the propeller disc, a similar calibre weapon being fitted in the vital dorsal position under the control of the bomb aimer and finally a 0.50-in gun in a power-operated turret, fired by the radio operator. Flight testing proceeded rapidly, and by the end of January 1942 the first production TBF-1s were already being issued to the US Navy. Like its Douglas predecessor, the Avenger was badly mauled when first exposed to the enemy at Midway in June 1942 – five of the six TBF-1s of VT-8 that were sent to attack the Japanese task force from Midway Island on 4 June were shot down prior to engaging their targets, and the

surviving aircraft returned to base with one of its gunners dead and the other seriously wounded. However, as its name suggested, the TBF/TBM meted out severe retribution on the Japanese over the next three years following this initial reversal.

One of the astounding features of the Avenger story is that the basic design of the aircraft changed very little during the course of its production life. This allowed vast quantities of Avengers to be built over a very short time scale – 2293 were produced between January 1942 and December 1943 alone! As with the Wildcat before, the US Navy's demand for Avengers soon outstripped Grumman's production capacity, so automotive giant General Motors (through the auspices of their Eastern Division) stepped into the breech and commenced producing the near identical TBM-1 from September 1942. Indeed, by the time the Avenger production line finally closed in June 1945 GM had built 7546 TBMs of various marks, a figure which far exceeded Grumman's own final build figure.

Aside from its extensive employment aboard virtually all US Navy carriers, the Avenger was also eagerly snapped up by the Fleet Air Arm, who desperately needed an advanced monoplane type to replace its venerable Swordfish and Albacore types. The first TBF-1s procured through Lend-Lease were issued to No 832 Sqn in January 1943 and renamed the Tarpon I after a large game fish found off the southern coast of America – this name lasted just 12 months, however, and the type soon reverted to its US Navy sobriquet of Avenger I. Over 1000 Avengers of several different marks proved the mainstay of the Fleet Air Arm through to VJ-Day.

▲ A TBM-1C is prepared for launch in the Pacific in 1943

▶ Avenger IIs of the Fleet Air Arm undertake a training sortie in 1944

'Screaming fighters, theirs and ours, were all over the place. Two of theirs got through the cover and were attacking us – my observer, George, was giving me a running commentary but they broke away without scoring any hits. Nearing the target now and the heavy ack-ack was opening up. Shell bursts galore just in front and very slightly below us, the brown puffs of smoke passing us in a flash – they can stay there, I thought. There was the target on the starboard side in the angle of the engine cowling and the wing. Come on, let's go, it's getting too hot up here and I feel very naked. Good, there we go and the wing leader peels off to starboard and down, followed by his Avengers.'

Lt Donald Judd, No 854 Sqn, HMS Illustrious, 1945

▲ TBM-3 Avenger

▶ TBM-3E Avenger and FG-1D Corsair

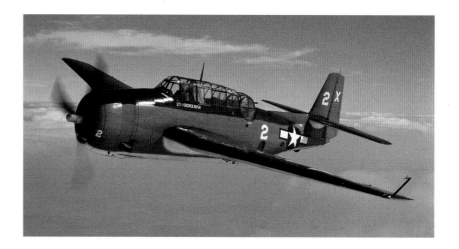

'I heard over the intercom from my gunner, "Rats, dead astern, closing fast". Then Don's voice, "He's firing at Mitch. Stand by to corkscrew", and then, "Corkscrew now". I rammed on full starboard rudder and pushed the stick down and hard to starboard. She responded immediately and then it was port rudder, stick back and to port to climb back up again before repeating the process. Don's voice came through again, "He's disappeared below us, but there is another one coming in on the starboard quarter". I said to the gunner, "Did you get a burst at him?", and he replied, "No, the gun's jammed after one round, and I'm still trying to clear it". I thought, "God, that's the last thing we needed. We'll be going into the dive in a minute when I shan't be able to take any avoiding action and we can do without one of those bastards on our tail". I yelled out, "Don can you get down to the belly gun so that at least we can squirt something at him?" Back came the reply, "OK Johnnie, I'm on my way". At the same time I was watching the rest of the formation, keeping my boys in nice and tight, looking at the target and searching for my particular part of it, and also trying to memorise the position of those bloody balloons.'
Lt Johnnie Baggs, No 820 Sqn, HMS Indefatigable, 1945

▶ TBM-3 Avenger and Corsair F4U-1

▲ TBM-3E Avenger

◀ TBM-3R COD Avenger

79797 97979

79797 97979

Avro

LANCASTER

'The Flight Commander stuck a form in my log-book and wrote on it: "Above the average". He told me I was going to Lancasters, and I felt a tingle of pleasure. Bomber Command had two other types of heavies – the Stirling and the Halifax – but I knew that the Avro Lancaster was the best of all bombers.' **Sgt Jack Currie, Heavy Bomber Conversion Unit, Church Broughton, 1943**

The Lancaster was to Bomber Command what the Spitfire was to Fighter Command – the definitive weapon of war, produced in overwhelming numbers in order to defeat the Axis scourge. Indeed, just as the famous Vickers-Supermarine design has overshadowed the exploits of other RAF fighters, so the Lancaster is today viewed as the *only* RAF heavy bomber of the conflict by the population of Great Britain, despite the fact that the Wellington, Stirling and Halifax all performed admirably over the hostile skies of occupied Europe.

Avro's superlative bomber was literally the 'phoenix that rose from the ashes' of the disastrous Manchester programme of 1940/41. This twin-engined machine was powered by two Rolls-Royce Vultures and boasted a layout near-identical to the Lancaster, but unlike the latter, it was plagued from the start by grave engine reliability problems. Just 202 were built, and of this number no less than 40 per cent were lost on operations and 25 per cent in accidents. Avro realised that their airframe design was essentially correct, but turned to Rolls-Royce and demanded access to the company's superlative Merlin. The Manchester had also been chronically underpowered, so Avro's chief designer, Roy Chadwick, ensured that its replacement would suffer no such problems and installed four Merlin Xs beneath the Lancaster's wing (which had had its span increased over that fitted to the Manchester by 12 ft to 102 ft).

The Lancaster prototype (a converted Manchester airframe) first flew on 9 January 1941, and its potential was soon realised during extensive flight trials. Following the

delivery of the second prototype (powered by new Merlin XX engines), the initial airframe was sent to No 44 Sqn for frontline evaluation, where both air- and groundcrew praised it highly. An order for 1070 bombers had been placed with Avro in mid-1941, and the first production machines emerged that October. The company's Chadderton and Yeadon factories soon became overwhelmed with work, so a large number of 'shadow' factories were employed fulfilling the Air Ministry's burgeoning orders. To ensure that enough engines were available to power the hundreds of Lancaster B Is rolling off the production line, Packard in America was licensed to build the Rolls-Royce powerplant – aircraft powered with these engines were designated B IIIs.

No 44 Sqn carried out the first operational sorties with the type in March 1942, although its existence was not revealed to the British public until August of that year. Undoubtedly the most famous raid undertaken by the Lancaster was the epic 'dambusting' mission performed by No 617 Sqn on 17 May 1943. The modifications carried out to the B IIIs involved, signalled the bomber's arrival as a precision attack instrument. Further raids by elite units saw the German battleship *Tirpitz* sunk by a direct hit from a 12,000-lb 'Tallboy' bomb and numerous concrete U-boat pens and viaducts knocked out by 22,000-lb 'Grand Slam' devices.

No less than 59 Bomber Command units saw active service with the Lancaster, flying 156,000 sorties and dropping 608,612 tons of high explosive bombs and 51 million incendiaries. Some 7377 airframes were built by the six factories devoted to Lancaster production, this number being split between five distinctive marks.

▲ An anonymous crew prepare for their 19th mission in late April 1943

▶ Lancaster B Is of No 44 Sqn head out on a mission in late 1942

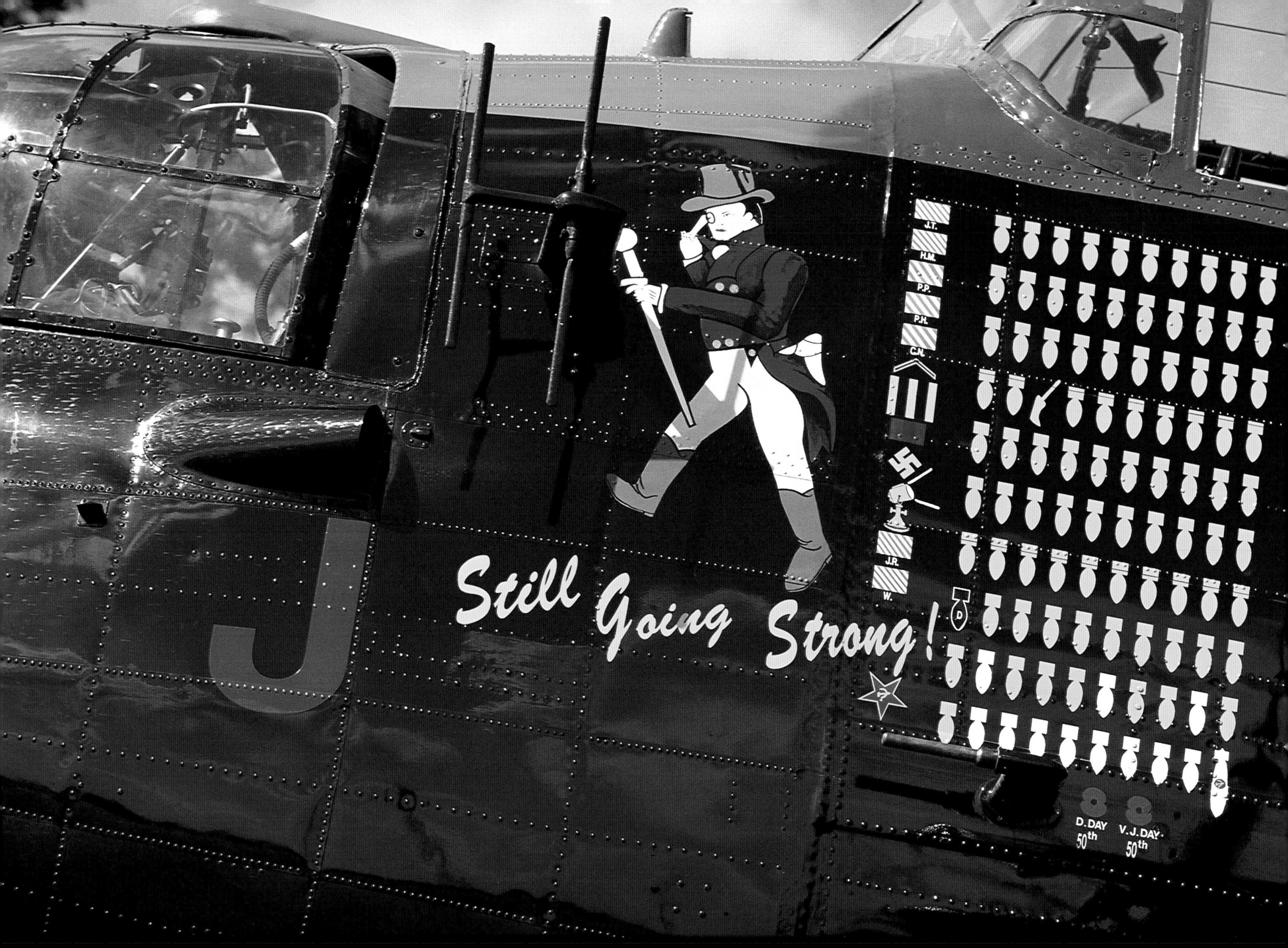
J
Still Going Strong!
J.T.
H.M.
P.P.
P.H.
C.N.
J.R.
W.
D.DAY 50th
V.J.DAY 50th

'Berlin, as I remember it, was not heavily defended in January 1943, but in November and December 1943 and January, February, March 1944 the defences were greatly improved. The sky above 20,000 ft was always lit up with flares, with a wall of flak up to 18,000 ft and nightfighters above that. I do remember one trip when we saw one Me 110 shoot down four Lancasters in about as many minutes, and we ourselves nearly crashed into a Me 109 as we left the target. He passed directly in front of me at a distance of no more than ten yards. The gunners were unable to get him in their sights as he was gone in seconds. I don't know who was more surprised – he or us! He was so close I could see him looking straight at me!'
Sgt Alan Wales, No 460 Sqn, Binbrook, 1944

◀ Lancaster B I(FE) ▲

'The target was partially covered by cloud when we got there, but we could see the ground target indicators laid by the Pathfinders, and were able to bomb them accurately. The sky was bright with fire and explosions as we closed our bomb doors, and with our load lightened, we turned for home with a great sense of elation. Suddenly my mid-upper gunner shouted over the intercom "Corkscrew port". As I threw our Lancaster into the initial diving turn I felt the thud of cannon shell in the port wing and the shudder and noise as both my gunners fired back. After a few violent corkscrew manoeuvres all went quiet. I took breath and mid-upper reported that he thought he had hit the Ju 88 which he had seen spiral away.'
Flg Off Michael Beetham, No 50 Sqn, Skellingthorpe, 1943

▲ A Lancaster B I taxies in on two engines after completing a night mission to Germany in early 1943

▶ Lancaster B I(FE)

'The flak got worse and worse. I hated the brilliant blue master searchlights, which began horizontal and then swiftly rotated up dead on target. The moment they latched on, one became coned by many others. This happened near Kiel. We were blinded, and then suddenly realised a nightfighter must be on us, because the flak had stopped. By luck one searchlight caught a nightfighter, and both gunners opened up on him. Maxi instantly did the tested S manoeuvre, and then went into a near-vertical dive. I pulled back the throttles. Sweat was pouring off Maxi's forehead, while I was picturing interrogation by the Gestapo. Maxi soon shouted "Help me pull back!" With both of us heaving, we managed to pull out at about 12,000 ft. Then I helped pour on power again. We survived.'

Wt Off 'Danny' Boon, No 625 Sqn, Kelstern, 1944

▲ Veteran Lancaster B I fitted with H2S radar

◀ Lancaster B I(FE)

Bell
P-63 KINGCOBRA

'Although I had heard many different stories about this "bird", both good and bad, from different pilots, I found the P-63 a fun aircraft to fly, with excellent visibility from the cockpit.' **Bill Littlejohn, Patterson Field, 1945**

Bell's P-39 of the early war years had introduced the concept of both the centrally-mounted powerplant and the tricycle undercarriage to single-engined fighters. That the aircraft lacked the true performance of other contemporary fighters at altitudes exceeding 12,000 ft was due to the Airacobra relying on the Allison V-1710 engine, which was fitted devoid of a turbocharger in the Bell fighter. Once it entered service in 1941, the wisdom of the decision to delete this essential device was quickly called into question. Indeed, so compromised was the aircraft's 'combatability' as a fighter interceptor that it was soon relegated to operating in the close support role in theatres where other aircraft could be employed to wrest air superiority from the enemy. Once assigned to attacking targets on the ground the P-39 came into its own, its nose-mounted 37 mm T-9 cannon and four 0.30-in machine-guns making for a deadly battery when ranged against vehicles and troop emplacements – the Soviets, in particular, appreciated the firepower and overall ruggedness of the Bell fighter, operating some 5000 from 1942 onwards.

Bell soon realised that improvements had to be made to the performance of the P-39, and instigated a programme to build a more powerful, and aerodynamically efficient, fighter. What they came up with bore a striking resemblance to the Airacobra, but was in fact a virtually all-new design that had a superior turn of speed at all altitudes. Known as the XP-63, and dubbed the Kingcobra, the new fighter relied significantly on modifications

incorporated into the XP-39E, a cancelled replacement for the P-39. However, unlike the still-born design, the XP-63 was more than just an Airacobra fuselage with new semi-laminar flow wings. The fighter was appreciably larger, and boasted an Allison V-1710-93 engine that could be boosted to 1500 hp in flight in the event of an emergency.

The prototype was first flown on 7 December 1942, and its subsequent evaluation proved to be so successful that production orders were placed that eventually saw some 3300 built in several different versions. However, by the time the first production examples began to reach the USAAF in October 1943, the performance of the P-51B, P-38H and P-47C had successfully filled the Air Force's requirement for a frontline fighter, so the aircraft was made available for lend-lease purchase, and the Soviets happily snapped up 2400 examples. A further 300 went to Free French units in the Mediterranean, but the primary customer – the USAAF – restricted their use of the Kingcobra to training units back in America. Some 300 were employed as gunnery 'targets' for pilots firing live ammunition in the form of frangible bullets, the Kingcobras being protected by the provision of a 1500-lb duralumin alloy skin, plus a variety of steel guards over exhaust stacks and the engine intake – bullet-proof glass was also employed in the canopy. The final variant in production at war's end was the P-63E, of which only 13 out of an order for 2930 had been delivered when the contract was cancelled following VJ-Day.

▲ P-63A seen at Edmonton in 1944 during its delivery flight to the Soviet Union

▶ P-63A marked up in standard USAAF late war markings

'The first ride went fairly well. At these settings, and at 1000 ft, airspeed indicated 410 to 420 mph, but it sure was a rough ride even when throttling back to 3000 rpm and 60" manifold pressure when going from wet to dry and dry to wet as severe vibration occurred. The aim of these tests was to get ten hours on the engine at 3260 rpm and 75", the purpose being to use the P-63C to possibly catch the Me 262.'

Bill Littlejohn, Patterson Field, 1945

▲ P-63A Kingcobra ▶

▲ P-63As at the Bell plant in 1944 prior to delivery to the Soviet Union

◀ P-63A Kingcobra

'During the third wet run, while the rpm was at 3260 and the manifold pressure was 75", severe vibration and backfires occurred. Even though the engine was behind me, pieces of cowling and ducting could be seen leaving the P-63. The intake manifold was blown apart and the backfire screens blown out the exhaust stacks, but luckily no fire occurred. The engine had to be changed. Several other flights were made, but our goal of ten hours wet time on the mighty Allison was never achieved.'

Bill Littlejohn, Patterson Field, 1945

▲ P-63A Kingcobra ▶

AIRCRAFT & PILOT GUIDE

Chapter 1

Pilots: *Nick Grey, Stuart Goldspink, Wg Cdr Dave Moss,*
Sqn Ldr 'Shiney' Simmons, Dan Griffith, Andy Sephton

Hurricane Mk XII RCAF 5711 *The Fighter Collection*
Hurricane Mk IIC PZ865 *Battle of Britain Memorial Flight*
Hurricane Mk IIC BE417 *Autokraft*
Sea Hurricane Mk IB Z7015 *Shuttleworth Collection*

Chapter 2

Pilots: *Ray Hanna, Stephen Grey, Mark Hanna, Nick Grey, Steve Hinton,*
Sir Tim Wallis, Flt Lt Paul Shenton, Tony Bianchi, Jonathan Whaley, Carl
Schofield, Andy Sephton, Andy Gent, Rudy Frasca, Charlie Brown, Jeff Ethell

Spitfire LF VB EP120 *The Fighter Collection*
Spitfire LF IXE ML417 *The Fighter Collection*
Spitfire FR XIVE MV293 *The Fighter Collection*
Spitfire Mk IA AR213 *Personal Plane Services*
Spitfire LF VC AR501 *The Shuttleworth Collection*
Spitfire Mk VIII MT719 The *Cavanaugh Museum*
Spitfire LF IXC MH434 *The Old Flying Machine Company*
Spitfire PR XI PL965 *The Old Flying Machine Company*
Spitfire LF XVIE TB863 *The Alpine Fighter Collection*
Spitfire LF XVIE RW382 *Historic Flying Ltd*
Spitfire FR XVIIIE TP280 *Frasca Simulation Ltd*
Spitfire PR XIX PS915 *Battle of Britain Memorial Flight*

Chapter 3

Pilot: *John Romain*

Blenheim Mk IV RCAF 10201 *The Aircraft Restoration Company*

Chapter 4

Pilots: *Rudy Frasca, Dick Hansen, Mark Hanna, John Lamont, Nick Grey*

P-40M 43-5802 *The Fighter Collection*
Kittyhawk Mk I AK905 *Frasca International*
Kittyhawk Mk I AK899 *Richard W Hansen*
P-40K 42-9733 *The Alpine Fighter Collection*

Chapter 5

Pilot: *Stephen Grey, Howard Pardue, Dick Hansen*

FM-2 Wildcat BuNo 86711 *The Fighter Collection*
F4F-3 Wildcat BuNo 12260 *Richard W Hansen*

Chapter 6

Pilot: *John Romain*

Lysander Mk IIIA *The Aircraft Restoration Company/Wessex Aviation*

Chapter 7

Pilots: *Eli Prothero, Pete Ford, Jim Porter, Ray Hillson, John Crocker,*
John Romain

B-25D Mitchell 43-3318 *The Fighter Collection*
B-25H Mitchell 43-4106 *Weary Warriors Squadron*
B-25J Mitchell 44-29507 *The Duke of Brabant Air Force*
B-25J Mitchell 44-30423 *Planes of Fame*

Chapter 8

Pilots: *Stephen Grey, Mark Hanna, John Romain, Vlado Lenoch, Brian Smith,*
Steve Noujaim, Anthony Buechler, Steve Hinton, Norman Lees, Pete Kynsey

P-51D Mustang 44-73149 *The Fighter Collection*
P-51A Mustang 43-6251 *Planes of Fame*
P-51D (CA-18) Mustang A68-192 *The Old Flying Machine Company*
P-51D Mustang 44-73877 *The Scandinavian Historic Flight*
P-51D Mustang 44-73656 *Vlado Lenoch*
P-51D Mustang 44-73339 *The Intrepid Aviation Company*
P-51D Mustang 44-73140 *Eastwind Inc*
P-51C Mustang 43-25147 *The Fighter Collection*

Chapter 9

Pilots: *Peter Henley, John Davies*

Mosquito T III RR299 *British Aerospace*

Chapter 10

Pilots: *Keith Sissons, 'Mac' MacKinney, Jim Jewell*

B-17G Flying Fortress 44-85784 *B-17 Preservation Trust Ltd*

Chapter 11

Pilot: *Steve Hinton*

A6M5 Zero 61-120 *Planes of Fame*

Chapter 12

Pilot: *John Maloney*

SBD-5 Dauntless BuNo 28536 *Planes of Fame*

Chapter 13

Pilots: *Steve Hinton, Hoof Proudfoot, Bruce Lockwood*

P-47D Thunderbolt *The Fighter Collection*
P-47G Thunderbolt 42-25234 *Planes of Fame*
P-47D Thunderbolt 44-90447 *Santa Monica Museum of Flying*

Chapter 14

Pilots: *Charlie Brown, Dave Southwood, Mark Hanna*

Bf 109G-2/Trop Nr 10639 *Imperial War Museum*
Bf 109G-10 *Hans Dittes/The Old Flying Machine Company*

Chapter 15

Pilots: *Nick Grey, Kevin Eldridge, Steve Hinton*

F6F-3 Hellcat BuNo 40467 *The Fighter Collection*
F6F-5 Hellcat BuNo 94473 *Planes of Fame*

Chapter 16

Pilots: *Hoof Proudfoot, Tom Middleton, Pete Kynsey, Ray Hanna*

FG-1D Corsair BuNo 88297 *The Fighter Collection*
F4U-1A Corsair BuNo 17995 *The Alpine Fighter Collection*
FG-1D Corsair BuNo 88391/NZ5648 *The Old Flying Machine Company*

Chapter 17

Pilots: *Hoof Proudfoot, Stephen Grey, Steve Hinton, Carl Schofield,*
Pete Kynsey

P-38J Lightning 42-67543 *The Fighter Collection*
P-38J Lightning 44-23314 *Planes of Fame*

Chapter 18

Pilots: *Jon Maloney, Ed Erikson, Rex Dovey, Rolf Meum, Dan Griffith*

TBM-3 Avenger BuNo 91264 *Planes of Fame*
TBM-3E Avenger BuNo 91110 *The Alpine Fighter Collection*
TBM-3E Avenger BuNo 53818 *The Polar Air Museum*
TBM-3R Avenger BuNo 53319 *Tony Haig-Thomas*

Chapter 19

Pilot: *Sqn Ldr Dave Buchanan, Flt Lt Jerry Ward*

Lancaster B I(FE) PA474 *Battle of Britain Memorial Flight*

Chapter 20

Pilot: *Nick Grey*

P-63A 42-69097 Kingcobra *The Fighter Collection*

Camera ship Pilots: *John Romain, Peter Monk, Dan Griffith, Susan Toner,*
Andy Gent, Gary Numan, John Webb, Mark Foster, Jon Hinton, Alan Walker,
Ed Haig-Thomas, Kevin Eldridge, Pete Ford, John Crocker, Hoof Proudfoot,
Eli Prothero, Brendan Walsh, Mark Hanna, Chris Fielder, Nigel Lamb,
David Jones, Nick Grey, Bob Thompson, Richard Verrall, Norman Lees

BIBLIOGRAPHY

The authors duly acknowledge that some of the brief extracts quoted within the text of this volume have come from the following books and periodicals, all of which are recommended as essential reading for anyone interested in piston-engined combat aircraft, and the men that flew them during World War 2.

Bauer D *Great American Fighter Aces* Motorbooks International 1992

Blackburn T *The Jolly Rogers* Orion Books 1989

Bowyer C *Mosquito at War* Ian Allan 1973

Boyington G *Baa Baa Blacksheep* Putnam 1958

Braham B *Scramble* William Kimber 1985

Brown E *Wings of the Navy* Jane's 1980

Christy J and Ethell J *P-40 Hawks at War* Ian Allan 1979

Christy J and Ethell J *P-38 Lightning at War* Ian Allan 1978

Currie J *Lancaster Target* New English Library 1977

Davis L *56th Fighter Group* Squadron/Signal Publications 1991

Deere A C *Nine Lives* Wingham Press 1991

Delve K *RAF Marham* Patrick Stephens Limited 1995

Dibbs J and Holmes T *Spitfire – Flying Legend* Osprey Aerospace 1996

Dibbs J and Holmes T *Hurricane – A Fighter Legend* Osprey Aerospace 1995

Duncan-Smith W *Spitfire into Battle* John Murray Ltd 1981

Dundas H *Flying Start* Stanley Paul 1988

Eadon S *Sakishima and back* Crécy 1995

Ethell J *Mustang – A documentary history* Jane's 1981

Freeman R A *B-17 Fortress at War* Ian Allan 1977

Freeman R A *Thunderbolt – A documentary history of the Republic P-47* Arms & Armour 1978

Freeman R A *Mustang at War* Ian Allan 1974

Franks N *Valiant Wings* Crécy 1994

Glines C V *The Doolittle Raid* Orion Books 1988

Goodson J A and Franks N *Over-Paid, Over-Sexed and Over Here* Wingham Press 1992

Goodson J A *Tumult in the Clouds* William Kimber 1983

Gunston B *Classic World War II Aircraft Cutaways* Osprey Aerospace 1995

Gunston B *"So Many"* W H Smith 1995

Hess W N *P-47 Thunderbolt at War* Ian Allan 1976

Judd D *Avenger from the Sky* William Kimber 1985

Kaplan P and Saunders A *Little Friends* Random House 1991

Knoke H *I Flew For The Führer* Time Life Books 1990

Lucas L *Wings of War* Hutchinson 1983

McDowell E R *49th Fighter Group* Squadron/Signal Publications 1989

Sakai S *Samurai* William Kimber 1959

Scott S R *Battle-Axe Blenheims* Alan Sutton 1996

Scutts J *Mustang Aces of the Eighth Air Force* Osprey Aerospace 1994

Scutts J *Mustang Aces of the Ninth and Fifteenth Air Force and the RAF* Osprey Aerospace 1995

Smith P C *Impact!* William Kimber 1981

Stanaway J *Peter Three Eight* Pictorial Histories Publishing Company 1986

Styling M *Corsair Aces of World War 2* Osprey Aerospace 1995

Taylor H A *Air International – Lysander article* July 1972 issue

Tillman B *Wildcat Aces of World War 2* Osprey Aerospace 1995

Tillman B *Hellcat Aces of World War 2* Osprey Aerospace 1996

Turner R E *Mustang Pilot* New English Library 1975

Various authors *In the Cockpit Flying the World's Great Aircraft* Studio Editions 1991

AUTHOR'S NOTE

Fifteen years ago my time was spent sitting in awe, endlessly leafing through books of images by such masters of their art as Charles Brown and Arthur Gibson. Who would have thought then, that the skies would be filled with over twenty different types of the great pistons, 30 plus aircraft - fighters, bombers and recce types from all nations, thundering through the heavens to form the finale of the 'Flying Legends' airshow at Duxford.

The passing of time has allowed me to produce a photographic book of these incredible machines, a compilation that takes in five years of my life. It's aim is simple - to get you as close as possible to these mighty beasts through the words of the men who flew them in combat, and the images from then and now. We have striven, with the contemporary images, to create a degree of authenticity that in some cases demanded the repainting of a number of airframes, to match the colours of their wartime counterparts more accurately. During the compilation of this book; one which forms a portfolio of my favourite images; I have been brought into contact with a superlative kind of human being, the machines draw on such spirits to make themselves exceptional. We owe a debt of thanks to these people - the owners and engineers who allow us to sense something of these awesome aircraft with their stubborn disregard for the near impossible. Thanks also to the pilots, who invariably cross over to the former - it is their skill and daring that allows me to capture these images, and whose displays harness the majesty of flight, in aircraft that are still on the edge of a

technology. Along the way fascinating stories have emerged, such as two P-40's flying together in 1996 which we discovered were built on the same day, in the same factory, back in 1943. Original pilots from the war meeting their contemporaries today, same aeroplane, same person, fifty years apart. We discussed the paintscheme accuracy for the A-model Mustang, (applied purely for this book), with Hollis Hills on the 'phone, shouting instructions across the hangar so that the markings matched exactly the aircraft in which he is credited with the first ever air combat victory in the North American thoroughbred. Imagine, a Battle of Britain ace walking onto Duxford airfield to see a Spitfire flying in his markings, 56 years on from his last flight there. He then strapped into a two-seater, to fly again himself, at 83 years old, when he was deemed too old to be a fighter pilot in 1940.

I must stress that the number of pages in this volume, and subsequent amount ascribed to each type, refer not to its historical importance - rather it is more indicative of the surviving number of airworthy examples, or the success of the relevant photosorties.

I would hope that this mix of words and pictures will be intoxicating enough for you to project yourself into the experience of others - and along the way to bear witness to the sacrifice of the period. Who knows what the next 15 years will bring. Keep watching the skies for 'Flying Legends'.

John M. Dibbs *November 1997*

I would also like to express thanks to: Stephen Grey, Nick Grey, Ray Hanna, Mark Hanna, John Romain, Graham Warner, Steve Hinton, Ed Maloney, Sir Tim Wallis, Ray Mulqueen, Ian Brodie, Jonathan Peel, Brian Lewis, John Lewis, David Henchie, Russ Snadden, Eli Sallingboe, Edwin Boshoff, Coert Munk, S/L Paul Day, Rudy Frasca, Brendan Walsh, Norman Lees, Tony Haig-Thomas, Anders Saether, Jim Porter, Tony Bianchi, Tom Allibone, Hans Dittes, David Price, Dan Griffith, Richard Verrall, Bruce Lockwood, Wally Fisk, Bob Monahan, Mike Johnson, Don Healey, Pete Brothers, Alex Vraciu, Geoffrey Page, George Unwin, Hollis Hills, Toru Sakurai, Masahide Ishizuka, Carl Anderson, Pete Rushen, Pippa Vaughan, Linda Spalding, Jeanne Frazer, Mel Hagger, Liam Harris, May Harris, Ruth Parker and Darren Baker.